JESUS

the **Aleph Tav**

James A. McMenis

xulon PRESS

CONTENTS

SPECIAL THANKS!

To my wife, Chrissy, for all you do every day that enables me to be the best I can be. I wouldn't be where I am without you. When God gave you to me, He gave me beyond all that I could have asked or envisioned. As a wife and mother, you are constantly amazing me. I love you and thank Him for you!

To my mom, Lola Byrd McMenis (1937-2008), and to my dad, Jessup "Al" McMenis (1930-1999), for never doubting my calling to preach the Gospel and for the undying love and support you have given me. I will be eternally grateful!

To the members and partners of Word of God Ministries, your support and encouragement fuels my passion for the ministry of His Word. I love you and thank God for you!

To Taylor Vlahakis and Naomi Lawler, you were both an amazing asset and made the editing experience an enjoyable process! You were truly Spirit-led. To all who assisted me in the writing of this book, I love and appreciate you!

Chapter 1

INTRODUCTION: THE VISION

And the Lord answered me, and said, Write the vision, and make it plain upon tables, that he may run that readeth it. For the vision is yet for an appointed time, but at the end it shall speak, and not lie: though it tarry, wait for it; because it will surely come, it will not tarry. Behold, his soul which is lifted up is not upright in him: but the just shall live by his faith. —HABAKKUK 2:2-4

Early in the ministry the Spirit of God gave me a specific message in regards to the Old Testament. He impressed on me that it is full of events, individuals, and stories that point directly to Jesus Christ. He began to open my eyes to the many pictures of Jesus that are inlaid throughout the Old Testament. I knew He wanted me to share these revelations with the assembly.

It was an exciting year as I ministered series after series from the Old Testament. I focused on the fact that the Old Testament is more than a record of God's creation and the history of His people. In a greater sense, it is also meant to direct our faith towards Jesus. I remember ministering messages like, "Jesus: Our Passover Lamb," "Jesus: Prophet, Priest and King," "Jesus: Our Jubilee," and "The Tabernacle: A Revelation of Jesus." It was in the heart of those messages that God planted the ultimate vision for the ministry He had given me, *"Preaching Jesus as the Manifested Word of God!"*

From that moment, to date, Word of God Ministries exists to use every available platform to declare that Jesus is the manifested Word of God. That may sound like a simple statement. It is my prayer and motive, that throughout the pages of this book, you realize that is not a simple statement but the very foundation of our faith!

I was 22 years old when the Lord led me to start a weekly Bible study that would eventually become Word of God Ministries. Shortly after its commencing, a pastor's wife I knew approached me. She was familiar with the weekly study and my teachings. She asked me why I put so much emphasis on "the Word." I remember hearing her say, *"All you talk about is the Word, the Word, the Word. Why don't you talk more about Jesus?"* I can remember my response just like it was yesterday. I said, *"Jesus is the Word!"*

At the time, I did not realize that the Lord was already laying the foundation for what would become a clear focus of the ministry years later. In those days individuals were always asking me what my vision was. I remember writing this lengthy vision statement that defined my beliefs and purpose in response. However, it wasn't until I spent a year of combing the Bible for Jesus, the Ancient of Days, that the vision truly became clear to me. From that moment, I have known with certainty what my call is and the purpose of the ministry the Lord has given me. The vision and purpose of my life is *"Preaching Jesus as the Manifested Word of God!"* It is truly amazing what I have witnessed since the Lord brought this clarity. Fasten your spiritual seat belts, because once you know the vision you can run with it!

After I was convicted with this vision I began to witness the Lord's supernatural blessing and favor upon Word of God Ministries. In 10 years, we literally went from 40 members to over 4,000. In that time, we've witnessed many come to know Christ and be baptized. Lives are becoming disciplined by the Word of God and bringing forth fruit that glorifies Him! There is power in the revelation of Jesus that comes from the Word of God!

It was right at the threshold of the ministry's growth when my dearest friend in life approached me about holding a weeklong revival type meeting. We had just completed two stages of our building plans and were getting ready to start a third in order to accommodate the growth. I had never been the type of pastor to advocate or call a "Revival" meeting. I had held weeklong meetings in the past, but my thought was that it is impossible to schedule a "revival." We can schedule a meeting and pray that it leads to a revival, but we can't schedule a revival itself.

I told my dear friend that I would pray about it. I prayed, and I do believe the Lord answered the same day. I scheduled a meeting that would begin on Sunday night and continue through Friday night. I called my friend Steve to tell him the news. "Brother Steve! I have booked the meeting!" I can remember that call vividly.

It was a very short turnaround from the time we set the dates to the start of the meeting. Immediately I went into prayer and meditation in the Word asking God for a specific message for the upcoming meeting. Within a day or two, I had a dear member and friend come by my office and leave a set of Hebrew Bibles. She and her husband felt like I would truly enjoy them and that they would be an awesome study tool. I had already been in the process of writing a book rooted in Genesis. I felt these Hebrew Bibles would truly help so I began to study them in depth. One Thursday night, I was up late preparing for my book and reading over the first volume of this new Hebrew/English Bible. Little did I know that the Lord was building something that would eventually become the vision and foundation of our ministry *"Preaching Jesus as the Manifested Word of God!"* On that Thursday night I literally saw something in the first line of Genesis 1:1 that arrested my attention and sent me on a journey that has led to the writing of a different book–the one you are reading now!

Brother Steve and I had scheduled a fishing trip the next day. Since I was meeting him at 5:30 a.m., I went to bed. Friday morning arrived. I grabbed my Hebrew Bibles and took off to meet Brother Steve. I could hardly wait to share with him what I had seen. I'll never forget it. I pulled into the Denny's parking lot to meet him and jumped out of my truck holding a stack of Hebrew Bibles. Excited, I said, *"Brother Steve! Man, I have got to show you something that I saw last night!"* If you know Brother

Steve, you know he loves to bass fish! I wish I could describe the look on his face when I handed him 4 volumes of the Bible in Hebrew!

I immediately opened up volume one to Genesis 1:1 and explained to him what I had discovered. *"Brother Steve, do you see that? That's Jesus! He's in Genesis 1:1!"* Ever the encourager, Brother Steve says, *"That's awesome Brother James! I guess you got your message for the upcoming meeting!"* He was right. Not only was it the message for that meeting, but also for the meetings that are now held annually at Word of God Ministries. That message would become one of the most rewarding revelations I have ever been honored and graced to receive. In the following chapters of this book, I look forward to sharing with you what I showed Brother Steve that Friday morning — the message I preached for five nights that summer and have preached at many conferences since. I can hardly wait for you to see Jesus, the Aleph Tav!

Chapter 2

IN THE BEGINNING
WAS THE WORD

In the beginning was the Word, and the Word was with
God, and the Word was God. —JOHN 1:1

John 1:1 has always been dear to me. I was so moved by it in the
early days of the ministry that we had this Scripture placed within
our ministry logo. I believe this verse is foundational when it comes to
understanding the revelation of Jesus. I think many have the idea that
there was a man named Jesus walking around Heaven before He was born
of a virgin in Bethlehem. They don't realize that *In the beginning was the
Word [Jesus].* Further study of this chapter really brings verse 1 to life.
Consider verse 14.

And the Word was made flesh, and dwelt among us, (and
we beheld his glory, the glory as of the only begotten of
the Father,) full of grace and truth. —JOHN 1:14

This verse sums up the Gospel story, "*The Word was made flesh, and dwelt among us.*" This is literally referring to Jesus being born (manifested) in the earth realm (See 1 John 1:2; 3:5, 8; 4:9). For the sake of study, let's look at verse 1 with verse 14.

VERSE 1:

[1] In the beginning was the Word, [2] and the Word was with God, [3] and the Word was God.

VERSE 14:

[1] And the Word was made flesh, [2] and dwelt among us, [3] (and we beheld his glory, the glory as of the only begotten of the Father,) full of grace and truth.

You will notice that I have broken each verse into three brackets. When you interlace the two, a beautiful revelation appears! Read the first bracket of verse 1 with the first bracket of verse 14. Allow me to illustrate this for you. Below I have joined the brackets of each of these verses together:

V.1   [1] In the beginning was the Word,

V.14   [1] And the Word was made flesh,

V.1   [2] and the Word was with God,

V.14   [2] and dwelt among us,

V.1   [3] and the Word was God,

V.14   [3] and we beheld his glory.

The message is clear. In the beginning was the Word. That Word was made flesh and was *tabernacled* in human form among us. This manifestation was glorious! This man, who was the Word made flesh, could be none other than the Son of the Living God!

> For there are three that bear record in heaven, the Father,
> the Word, and the Holy Ghost: and these three are one.
> —1 JOHN 5:7

We must realize that Jesus is the manifested Word of God! You cannot separate Jesus from the Word. Jesus is the Word. Revelation 13:19 declares, *"His name is called The Word of God."*

> ¹That which was from the beginning, which we have
> heard, which we have seen with our eyes, which we have
> looked upon, and our hands have handled, of the Word
> of life; ²(For the life was manifested, and we have seen
> it, and bear witness, and shew unto you that eternal life,
> which was with the Father, and was manifested unto us.
> —1 JOHN 1:1-2

> ²²Lord possessed me in the beginning of his way, before
> his works of old. ²³I was set up from everlasting, from
> the beginning, or ever the earth was. ²⁴When there
> were no depths, I was brought forth; when there were

no fountains abounding with water. ²⁵Before the mountains were settled, before the hills was I brought forth: ²⁶While as yet he had not made the earth, nor the fields, nor the highest part of the dust of the world. ²⁷When he prepared the heavens, I was there: when he set a compass upon the face of the depth: ²⁸When he established the clouds above: when he strengthened the fountains of the deep: ²⁹When he gave to the sea his decree, that the waters should not pass his commandment: when he appointed the foundations of the earth: ³⁰Then I was by him, as one brought up with him: and I was daily his delight, rejoicing always before him; ³¹Rejoicing in the habitable part of his earth; and my delights were with the sons of men. —PROVERBS 8:22-31

To truly begin to walk in the depth of who Jesus is, we must come to see Him through the lens of His Word. There are three things that we need to establish from John 1:1, 14 before we move forward: First, *"In the beginning was the Word."* Secondly, *"the Word was with God."* Thirdly, *"the Word was made flesh."* Once you grasp these truths, you will know with all assurance that Jesus truly is who He says He is. He is the Messiah, the Christ, the manifested Word, and the Son of the Living God!

And unto the angel of the church of the Laodiceans write; These things saith the Amen, the faithful and true witness, the beginning of the creation of God. — REVELATION 3:14

[16]For by him were all things created, that are in heaven, and that are in earth, visible and invisible, whether they be thrones, or dominions, or principalities, or powers: all things were created by him, and for him: [17]And he is before all things, and by him all things consist. — COLOSSIANS 1:16-17

Here, we see Jesus called the "*beginning of the creation of God*" and that "*all things were created by Him*" and that "*He is before all things.*" Ephesians 3:9 declares that all things were created by Jesus Christ! Throughout Scripture a consistent connection between Jesus and the creation can be seen. With that in mind, let's consider how God created the heavens and the earth. We see clearly that Jesus [the Word] was the vehicle of Creation, but we must consider how this is possible. Let's turn our attention to the opening chapter of the Book of the Beginning — Genesis.

Notice the following verses in Genesis 1:3, 6, 9, 11, 14, 20, 24, 26, 31

V.3   And God said, Let there be light: and there was light.

V.6   And God said...

V.9   And God said...

V.11   And God said...

V.14 And God said...

V.20 And God said...

V.24 And God said...

V.26 And God said...

V.31 And God saw...

Genesis records that when God created the earth, He did it through the avenue of His Word! I love how the chapter ends; *"God saw."* What did God see? He saw everything He said! God's words are so powerful, and so full of creative faith, that He has the ability to speak and immediately see the manifestation of what He spoke into existence. All things, both visible and invisible, were created by the power of His Word! With this understanding, reading John 1:1 opens a new perspective of Jesus, the Word. Truly, *"In the beginning was the Word."*

> All things were made by him; and without him was not
> any thing made that was made. —JOHN 1:3

Jesus, through the form of the Word, is the author and beginning of all things. Through the faith-substance of His word, all things were created (Hebrews 11:3). God transported His creative faith through the avenue of His Word. He literally formed, framed, and assembled all things that exist both naturally and spiritually into existence by speaking His Word.

Some within the science community may finally be catching up with yet another truth from God's Word. A friend of mine recently shared a video link with me by Jason Silva entitled "The World Is Made Of Language." This video explores the idea that the world is made from words (language). I stand in the faith that the world was made from language — the very breath and word of God!

> ⁶By the word of the Lord were the heavens made; and all the host of them by the breath of his mouth.
> ⁹For he spake, and it was done; he commanded, and it stood fast. —PSALMS 33:6, 9

> ¹Praise ye the Lord. Praise ye the Lord from the heavens: praise him in the heights.
> ⁵Let them praise the name of the Lord: for he commanded, and they were created. —PSALMS 148:1, 5

> I have made the earth, and created man upon it: I, even my hands, have stretched out the heavens, and all their host have I commanded. —ISAIAH 45:12

This revelation leads to a deeper conclusion. If Creation (as recorded in Genesis) itself is the result of His Word, then words would have had to existed before Creation. Have you ever considered that God's first creation was words? I believe that we have been contaminated with this idea that words — and the ability to speak — are something that have evolved over time. We've had this idea that the first man was some cave-man creature walking around beating on his chest and mumbling sounds. That's not true at all. In reality, the Bible records that man was made intelligent and with the ability to speak, communicate, and command. One of Adam's first assignments was to name every species of animal (Genesis 2:19-20). God gave him this intelligence and language —God is the author of words!

Can you see God forming words to be the container and vehicle in which He would deliver His plan? I believe that Creation, God's plan for mankind, salvation, and His ultimate will have been delivered through the power of His Word. Hebrews 1:3 says that God upholds all things by the word of His power!

THE WORD WAS MADE FLESH

And the Word was made flesh, and dwelt among us, (and we beheld his glory, the glory as of the only begotten of the Father,) full of grace and truth. —JOHN 1:14

In the beginning (before time as we know it), Jesus existed as the Word. The Word became flesh (when Jesus was conceived in the womb of a virgin). The Word was with God but came to dwell among us (God sent His Son to save). The Word was God and therefore we beheld His glory!

What is '*glory*'? Hebrews 1:3 describes glory as the expressed image of God. It is the heavyweight of God's presence. The glory of God is the manifestation of God's presence! In essence, it is the very existence of God revealed.

There's a difference between being present and manifesting your presence. You could be in the same room as an old friend from college and not know it. Imagine that old friend starts playing the piano. You might say afterwards, *"I didn't know you were in town!"* Then you might say, *"I didn't know you played the piano!"* The friend's presence and abilities were made manifest. That's the way we must see God. His Word says that we cannot escape His presence (Psalms 139:7). God is omnipresent—He is everywhere! There is a difference between Him being present and Him manifesting His presence.

Jesus came as the manifested Word of God to reveal the heart, love, power and nature of God to man. Many view the Bible as a revelation of God's power, when it is actually a revelation of His love; it is by His love that we see His power! God's Word reveals who He is. When Jesus was manifested in the earth that was God disclosing who He is!

The glory of God has always existed in the Word. God's Word is a container of His glory. Just as we use our words to convey who we are to others, the Word portrays the essence of God. When the Word became flesh through the womb of a virgin, God was depositing Himself, His glory, into human flesh—the God-man, Jesus. He manifested His glory from one form to another—from the Word to flesh. Thus the Word of God is the original container of the glory of God. When *"the word was made flesh... we beheld His glory."*

Jesus was not merely some good man who walked this earth and taught us how to love one another. Jesus was born in the earth as the only begotten Son of God. He is the Messiah, the Christ, and the Savior of the world! He is the manifested Word of God! There were over 300 prophecies concerning Him in the Old Testament! Everything about Him was declared before He was ever born in the earth. His lineage, birthplace, forerunner, teachings, and the details of His betrayal are all foretold in the Old Testament. The price He would be betrayed for and what would come of that money are declared in the Old Testament. His death, the means of His death in every detail, His resurrection, and His return are all recorded in the prophecy of the Old Testament. These are just a few of the hundreds of prophecies and descriptions of Him that were recorded in the Old Testament. These words were written by prophets, priests, kings, and shepherds as they were moved by the Spirit of God. These prophecies span nearly 1500 years. They were written by men who never met nor shared one another's notes, yet their writings portray perfect harmony. The Old Testament is Jesus concealed and the New Testament is Jesus revealed! No wonder Jesus said:

> Search the scriptures; for in them ye think ye have eternal life: and they are they which testify of me. —JOHN 5:39

WE BEHELD HIS GLORY

The Gospels record His birth, life, teachings, miracles, judgment, crucifixion and resurrection. They truly portray that *"the Word was made flesh, and dwelt among us"* (John 1:14). This life that was manifested

23

conveyed the light of the glory and nature of God. Even with His first miracle, we read:

> This beginning of miracles did Jesus in Cana of Galilee, and manifested forth his glory; and his disciples believed on him. —JOHN 2:11

Jesus worked His first miracle at a wedding. The Scripture above says that when He worked this miracle, it manifested His glory (John 2:11). It's like the old friend from college who played the piano and revealed a talent that you were unaware of. When Jesus began to work miracles, it revealed that He was more than just a man! The glory of God was witnessed in the person, the man—the human flesh of Jesus Christ!

In John 17, just before Jesus gave His life for ours, we read of a prayer that He prayed to the Father. In verse 5, Jesus asks the Father for something that we need to pay attention to. We know according to John 1:1, 14 that the Word of God is the original container of the glory of God. We also discovered that same glory was transferred when the Word was made flesh. With that in mind, let us look at Jesus' prayer:

> And now, O Father, glorify thou me with thine own self **with the glory which I had with thee before the world was.** —JOHN 17:5 (emphasis added)

What an amazing statement and request! Jesus asked the Father for the glory He had before the world was. In other words, He is asking His Father to put Him back into His original form of glory. Where was the glory before the world was? It was in the Word! Remember, the glory is the expressed image of God. It is God's presence manifested or revealed. Jesus is asking that the glory be transferred back into its original container. Why would He do this? I believe it is because He knows that His body is about to be offered unto death. The Bible teaches in Romans 6:4 that Jesus was raised from the dead by the glory! It was going to be His Word (filled with the glory) that would raise His body of flesh to life!

At some point in your life you may have petitioned God as Moses did in Exodus 33:18, *"Show me Your glory."* Well, I am here to tell you right now that His glory is in His Word. You may have prayed, *"Jesus, I want more of You."* The answer to more of Jesus is more of His Word! His Word is the container of His glory. There can be no true revelation of Jesus outside the avenue of His Word. This is the method in which He has chosen to make Himself known.

> [1]In the beginning was the Word, and the Word was with God, and the Word was God.
> [14]And the Word was made flesh, and dwelt among us, (and we beheld his glory, the glory as of the only begotten of the Father,) full of grace and truth.

⁵And now, O Father, glorify thou me with thine own self with the glory which I had with thee before the world was. —JOHN 1:1, 14; 17:5

I believe the most powerful example in Scripture of how Jesus is revealed to us through the Word of God is found in Luke 24 when Jesus met the disciples on the road to Emmaus. Through the understanding we have just gained by studying John 1:1, 14, you are now ready to see this powerful example of this truth. Let's read the account in Luke 24.

¹³And, behold, two of them went that same day to a village called Emmaus, which was from Jerusalem about three-score furlongs. ¹⁴And they talked together of all these things which had happened. ¹⁵And it came to pass, that, while they communed together and reasoned, Jesus himself drew near, and went with them. ¹⁶But their eyes were holden that they should not know him. ¹⁷And he said unto them, What manner of communications are these that ye have one to another, as ye walk, and are sad? ¹⁸And the one of them, whose name was Cleopas, answering said unto him, Art thou only a stranger in Jerusalem, and hast not known the things which are come to pass there in these days? ¹⁹And he said unto them, What things? And they said unto him, Concerning Jesus of Nazareth, which was a prophet mighty in deed and word before God and

all the people: ²⁰And how the chief priests and our rulers delivered him to be condemned to death, and have crucified him. ²¹But we trusted that it had been he which should have redeemed Israel: and beside all this, to day is the third day since these things were done. ²²Yea, and certain women also of our company made us astonished, which were early at the sepulchre; ²³And when they found not his body, they came, saying, that they had also seen a vision of angels, which said that he was alive. ²⁴And certain of them which were with us went to the sepulchre, and found it even so as the women had said: but him they saw not. ²⁵Then he said unto them, O fools, and slow of heart to believe all that the prophets have spoken: ²⁶Ought not Christ to have suffered these things, and to enter into his glory? ²⁷**And beginning at Moses and all the prophets, he expounded unto them in all the scriptures the things concerning himself.** —LUKE 24:13-27 (emphasis added)

We read here how the resurrected Savior appeared before His disciples. Yet the Bible says that they did not recognize Him. Why? The answer is that He was in His resurrected form. Notice what Jesus used to reveal His glory to His disciples. *"And beginning at Moses and all the prophets, he expounded unto them **in all the scriptures the things concerning himself"** (Luke 24:27, emphasis added). Jesus used the Word of God to reveal to His own disciples the glory of who He is. These were the same people who had spent the previous three years with Him. If Jesus used *"all the scriptures"* to reveal His glory to His own disciples, how much more do we need the Word in order to see the glory?

There is another example of Jesus being revealed through Scripture recorded in the Book of Acts:

> [29]Then the Spirit said unto Philip, Go near, and join thyself to this chariot. [30]And Philip ran thither to him, and heard him read the prophet Esaias, and said, Understandest thou what thou readest? [31]And he said, How can I, except some man should guide me? And he desired Philip that he would come up and sit with him. [32]The place of the scripture which he read was this, He was led as a sheep to the slaughter; and like a lamb dumb before his shearer, so opened he not his mouth: [33]In his humiliation his judgment was taken away: and who shall declare his generation? for his life is taken from the earth. [34]And the eunuch answered Philip, and said, I pray thee, of whom speaketh the prophet this? of himself, or of some other man? [35]**Then Philip opened his mouth, and began at the same scripture, and preached unto him Jesus.** —ACTS 8:29-35 (emphasis added)

This man believes on Jesus, is baptized, and then returns to his homeland with rejoicing (verses 37-39), all because Jesus had just revealed Himself through the avenue of His Word!

I remember shortly after my salvation that I went through a deep depression. I had been serving the Lord faithfully at church. I was doing everything from mowing the church lawn to driving the Sunday school bus. Yet in that same time frame, I got really discouraged by some things that were happening in my life. I got so discouraged that I literally lost my desire for living. One night I was up late feeling broken. About 1:30 in the morning I began to offer my complaint to God in prayer. I felt like I had served Him faithfully but that He had not been good to me. I remember hearing these words in my heart, *"You've not been serving me, you've served man. You don't know me."* I immediately asked God to reveal Himself to me. I wanted to know Him! I sensed an immediate desire to open my Bible. That moment changed my life forever! I opened His Word and began to see things that I had never seen before. I tell everyone that was like getting *"born again"* — again! All that my life needed was a revelation of the One in whom I wanted to know, to love, and to honor. That revelation came to me through His Word at a time that I desperately needed it and it left me forever changed!

Since that time in my life I have personally witnessed countless lives changed through the revelation of Jesus that comes when people begin to see Him in the glory of His Word. When I take time to reflect over my own walk of faith, and even before, I can see how the Lord has always led me to His Word. One day I was walking to get on my bus to head home from school when a Gideon handed me a little green New Testament. I was in the 5th grade. I can remember reading it all the time and even using spare time in class to read it to other class mates. This is when I gained the title *"Brother James."* At this point in my life, my parents didn't take me to church. I had not yet made a personal decision to accept Christ. I remember my dad complaining about preachers and how they *"didn't use the Bible anymore."* Both my parents believed in Christ. Later, at the age of seventeen, my family started attending church and I accepted Jesus as Lord and Savior. I received a new Bible as a gift when I was baptized. I remember thinking, *"I am going to finally learn the Bible!"*

The Gideon's New Testament, the Bible at my baptism, opening my Bible to discover God that night of intense depression, the Hebrew Bibles that were given to me early in ministry, all were ways that God was leading me to a walk with Him—a walk through the glory of His Word!

It is by His Word that we begin to know the glory of who He is! *"For of him, and through him, and to him, are all things: to whom be glory for ever. Amen"* (Romans 11:36). With all that we have studied so far, notice the following:

> [25]Now to him that is of power to stablish you according to my gospel, and the preaching of Jesus Christ, according to the revelation of the mystery, which was kept secret since the world began,

²⁶But now is made manifest, and by the scriptures of the prophets, according to the commandment of the everlasting God, made known to all nations for the obedience of faith: ²⁷To God only wise, be glory through Jesus Christ for ever. Amen. —ROMANS 16:25-27

These verses portray everything that we have studied from John 1:1, 14. Notice the wording, *"since the world began."* Compare that to John 1:1, *"in the beginning was the Word."* Notice, *"made manifest, and by the scriptures of the prophets."* Compare that to John 1:14, *"and the Word was made flesh."* Notice, *"be glory through Jesus Christ,"* and compare that to John 1:14, *"and we beheld His glory."* The message throughout the New Testament is consistent and clear. Jesus is the manifested Word of God!

In the beginning, the glory of God was placed in the container of His Word. That Word was made flesh in the person of Jesus Christ. The glory of God was revealed through the words and acts of Jesus. He has once again re-deposited His glory into the vessel of His Word thus carrying the power, revelation and manifestation of all that He is to those who will receive it!

Some years ago, when the ministry was young, I was producing a weekday radio program. One evening I received a call from a listener in Augusta, Georgia. He was struggling in his walk of faith. He told me that He had been praying to his picture of Jesus that was hung in his house but didn't think the Lord was responding. I encouraged him to open the Bible and come to know Jesus through His Word! If you are struggling to know Him, if you feel like your faith is limited and your vision obscure, open His Word! The glory of God is revealed in Jesus, the Word of God!

THE WORD WAS GOD

An amazing point that must not be overlooked in John 1:1 is the statement, "and the Word was God." I was visiting with a friend from Israel about the oneness that Jesus has with the Word —how He is the manifested Word of God. We were talking about the Word being the fulness and power of God. He then informed me that in the *Targumim* (the Aramaic translations of the original Hebrew Scriptures), the words "God" and "Lord" were translated in many cases as "the Word." The *targumim* was likely in circulation in the time of Jesus. These translations, or *explanations*, existed as a result of the Babylonian exile that stripped most Jews from their native language of Hebrew. (See Nehemiah 8:6-8; Ezra 4:18). The exiled Jews had adopted Aramaic and it became their language. Therefore, the rabbis had to translate the Hebrew to Aramaic when they read from the Hebrew Scriptures. He informed me that a verse was read in Hebrew followed by the same verse in Aramaic. What's amazing is that the "Word of God" (in Aramaic) was the substitution for "God" or "Lord" in many places in the Hebrew Scriptures.

Below are just a few examples taken from a *targum* known as "Targum Pseudo-Jonathan" (emphasis added):

When they heard the sound of the **Word of the Lord God** walking about in the garden as the day was ending, then Adam and his wife hid from before the Lord God in the midst the trees of the garden. —GENESIS 3:8-9

Then he said, "I heard the sound of your **Word** in the garden, and I was afraid, for I am naked. Because I transgressed the commandment that you commanded me, so I hid on account of shame." —GENESIS 3:10

Male and female he created them, and he blessed them in the name of his **Word** and called their name Adam on the day when they were created. —GENESIS 5:2

And those who were going in, male and female of all flesh, entered just as the Lord God had commanded him, and the **Word of the Lord** shut the door of the ark after him. —GENESIS 7:16

Then the Lord remembered Noah by his **Word**, and every wild animal and every domesticated animal that was with him in the ark, and the Lord made a spirit of mercy pass over the earth, and the waters subsided. —GENESIS 8:1

Then God said, "This is the sign of the covenant that I will make between my **Word** and you, and between every living creature that is with you, for the generations: I have set my bow in the cloud, and it will be a sign of the covenant between my **Word** and the earth. — GENESIS 9:12-13

[15]And I will remember my covenant that is between my **Word** and between you, and between every living creature among all flesh, and the waters will never again become a flood to destroy all flesh. [16]And the bow will be in the cloud, and I will see it for a reminder of an eternal covenant between the **Word of God** and every living creature among all flesh that is on the earth." [17]Then God said to Noah, "This is the sign of the covenant that I have established between my **Word** and the word of all flesh that is on the earth." —GENESIS 9:15-17

And I will establish my covenant between my **Word** and you, and I will increase you very much." —GENESIS 17:2

And I will establish my covenant between my **Word** and you, and your descendants after you, throughout their generations, for an eternal covenant, to be God to you and to your descendants after you, —GENESIS 17:7

This is my covenant that you shall keep between my **Word** and you, and your descendants after you, to circumcise every male of yours, if he has no father to circumcise him. And you shall circumcise the flesh of your foreskin, and it shall be a sign of the covenant between my Word and you. —GENESIS 17:10-11

[2]AND the Lord spake with Mosheh, and said to him, I am the Lord who revealed Myself to thee in the midst of the bush, and said to thee, I am the Lord. And I was revealed unto Abraham, and to Izhak, and to Jakob, as EI-Shaddai; but My Name Ye-ya, as it discovereth My Glory, was not known to them. [JERUSALEM. [3]And the Lord was revealed in **His Word** unto Abraham, to Izhak, and to Jakob, as the God of Heaven; but **the Name of the Word of the Lord** was not known. to them.] — EXODUS 6:1-3

[7]and I will proclaim the Name of the Lord before thee, and I will be gracious to whom I will be gracious, and have mercy on whom I will have mercy. And He said, Thou canst not see the Face of My Shekinah; for no man can see Me and abide alive. And the Lord said, Behold, there is a place prepared before Me, and thou shalt stand upon the rock, and it shall be, when My Glory passeth, I will

put thee in a cavern of the rock, and **My Word** shall over-shadow thee until I have passed; and I will take away the **word** (dibberath) of My Glory, and thou shalt see that which is after Me, [8]but My Aspect [9]shall not be seen. — EXODUS 30:7-9

My point in sharing this is to further verify the oneness that God has with His Word. From the beginning, God has always revealed Himself through His Word. In a culture where so many are ignorant of the Bible, it is no wonder that we are seeing a shift in society away from the character of God. We as believers must make a decision to get back to the source that reveals the very heart, nature, and essence of God — that is His Word! *"In the beginning was the Word, and the Word was with God, **and the Word was God"** (John 1:1, emphasis added).

Chapter 3

IN THE BEGINNING
WAS ALEPH TAV

[17]Think not that I am come to destroy the law, or the prophets: I am not come to destroy, but to fulfil. [18]For verily I say unto you, Till heaven and earth pass, one jot or one tittle shall in no wise pass from the law, till all be fulfilled. —MATTHEW 5:17-18

I started preaching the Word at the age of 17. For most of my walk of faith, I never fully comprehended what Jesus meant in Matthew 5:18. How many truly know what a jot or tittle is? I always compared it to the dotting of the "i" and the crossing of the "t." It's a loose comparison at best. Truthfully, the jot and tittle aren't really comparable to the English alphabet because there is so much more to be gleaned from the letters in their original Hebrew form.

Jesus' comments about the *jot* and *tittle* come on the heels of an important statement. "*Think not that I am come to destroy the law, or the prophets: I am not come to destroy, but to fulfill"* (Matthew 5:17). Jesus was further confirming that He is the manifested Word of God. We covered this in the previous chapter. I would like to expound on it a little more. Jesus was declaring that He came to fulfill all of the laws and all of the prophecies. Considering that there were over 300 prophecies, types and shadows that pointed to the Christ, that is a major statement. Aside from the Psalms and Proverbs, the Old Testament basically contains the Law and Prophets.

There are 39 books in the Old Testament. That is a very interesting number when you consider the spiritual importance of the number 40. In Scripture, "forty" represents fulfillment or something being completed or made whole. There are countless examples of major Biblical events happening in increments of 40. The flood of Noah lasted 40 days. Scripture declares it rained for 40 days and nights. Moses received the Ten Commandments after spending 40 days on Mount Sinai. Israel wandered in the wilderness for 40 years. The Prophet Elijah isolated himself after a major victory for 40 days. The reign of King David lasted for 40 years. David's son, King Solomon, reigned for 40 years. Jonah declared a 40-day prophecy to the people of Nineveh. Jesus prayed and fasted for 40 days. And after His crucifixion, burial, and resurrection, Jesus walked the earth for 40 days before His ascension. Not only does this number signify fulfillment, but it also has significance in Jewish culture. According to Jewish tradition, one complete generation was measured by the span of 40 years.

It is no coincidence that God ended the Old Testament with only 39 books. I believe it is because the Law and Prophets could not be fulfilled without Christ! Jesus shows up in the New Testament, literally in the 40th book, Matthew. The Gospel of Matthew records 16 occasions where Jesus said or did something so that the Scriptures might be *"fulfilled."* He made it clear to the Old Testament scholars that the writings with which they were so familiar were written about Him. *"Search the scriptures; for in them ye think ye have eternal life: and they are they which testify of me"* (John 5:39). Jesus is the fulfillment of all Law and Prophecy!

> Then said I, Lo, I come: in the volume of the book it is written of me. —PSALMS 40:7

> Then said I, Lo, I come (in the volume of the book it is written of me,) to do thy will, O God. —HEBREWS 10:7

There is a clear pattern in the New Testament of the Old Testament Scriptures being fulfilled by Christ. The New Testament writers understood the weight of this. In essence, it proves the point that Jesus was not some self-proclaimed prophet. God ordained Jesus to fulfill these prophecies that were recorded before His birth so that the world would know He was not like any other man-made idol, false prophet, or false god. He was, in fact, the one and only Son of God—sent by God to finish a work that only He could finish.

But those things, which God before had shewed by the mouth of all his prophets, that Christ should suffer, **he hath so fulfilled**. —ACTS 3:18 (emphasis added)

To him give all the prophets witness, that through his name whosoever believeth in him shall receive remission of sins. —ACTS 10:43 (emphasis added)

And when they had fulfilled all that was written of him, they took him down from the tree, and laid him in a sepulchre. —ACTS 13:29 (emphasis added)

²And Paul, as his manner was, went in unto them, and three sabbath days **reasoned with them out of the scriptures**, ³Opening and alleging, that Christ must needs have suffered, and risen again from the dead; and that this Jesus, whom I preach unto you, is Christ —ACTS 17:2,3 (emphasis added)

³For I delivered unto you first of all that which I also received, how that **Christ died for our sins according to the scriptures**; ⁴And that he was buried, and that he rose again the third day according to the scriptures: —I CORINTHIANS 15:3, 4 (emphasis added)

(Which he had promised afore by his prophets in the holy scriptures,) —ROMANS 1:2 (emphasis added)

Let's now look at the second part of Jesus' statement. *"For verily I say unto you, Till heaven and earth pass, **one jot** or **one tittle** shall in no wise pass from the law, till all be fulfilled"* (Matthew 5:18 emphasis added). The *"jot"* is actually the smallest letter of the Hebrew alphabet. The *"tittle"* is a small apex or crown that appears on 8 of the 22 Hebrew letters. Jesus was not only placing emphasis on the fulfillment of the Word, but He was emphasizing the very letters that make up the Word!

ALPHA AND OMEGA

Chances are you have probably heard the phrase *"Alpha and Omega."* It is a name that represents Jesus. This is how He referred to himself, *"I am Alpha and Omega..."* (Revelation 1:8, 11, 21:6, 22:13). What does it mean? *"Alpha"* and *"Omega"* are the first and last letters of the Greek alphabet. What was Jesus really saying? He was, again, alluding to the fact that He is the fulfillment of all Scripture.

Consider this: The entirety of Scripture is made up of words. Words don't exist without letters. Hebrew letters are unique in nature. Each letter has its own meaning and significance. The Scriptures were originally written in Hebrew and later translated to Greek. Jesus was saying that He is not only the fulfillment of the Word but He is also the fulfillment of the letters used to publish the Word. We will soon take a much closer look at this. For now, consider the fact that Jesus called himself Alpha and Omega, the completion of everything written in scripture from the first letter to the last letter.

On three occasions the Apostle John, by the Spirit of God, writes that Jesus appeared unto him declaring that He was *"Alpha and Omega."* He could have simply said, *"I am the first and the last,"* but Jesus chose to make the distinction by using the letters *"Alpha and Omega."* This distinguishing between words and letters is important. Jesus is not only declaring that He is the Word, but that He is the very letters that are used to form the Word!

There is something we need to address here. The New Testament was translated in Greek. Though it is likely that Jesus spoke Greek and even Latin, He certainly spoke Hebrew. At the age of twelve there is evidence of Him speaking Hebrew in discussing the Torah (the written Law) with the religious leaders of that day (Luke 2:39-52). He would have spoken to the Samaritan woman at the well in Hebrew (John 4:4-26). Hebrew was the language of the Passover blessing (Matthew 26:26-30). The inscription on the cross was written in Hebrew (John 19:20). From the cross we see Him speaking Hebrew (Matthew 27:46). After His resurrection and ascension, Jesus addressed Paul in the Hebrew tongue. *"And when we were all fallen to the earth, I heard a voice speaking unto me, **and saying in the Hebrew tongue**, Saul, Saul, why persecutest thou me? it is hard for thee to kick against the pricks"* (Acts 26:14, emphasis added).

Hebrew is a divine language — it is the language of the Jews, God's holy nation. Greek is the language of the New Testament translation.

There is no reason to believe that Jesus appeared to the Apostle John on the Isle of Patmos and spoke Greek. If He had, there would be no need for translation. Greek is the translated language; therefore, we see it recorded, *"Alpha and Omega."*

I believe with everything in me that Jesus spoke to John in Hebrew and said, *"I am ALEPH and TAV."* ALEPH and TAV are the first and last letters of the Hebrew alphabet. As we advance in this study you will discover why this is so important.

ALEPH TAV

As I shared in the opening chapter of this book, some years ago I was reading Genesis 1:1 in a Hebrew Bible and noticed something very interesting. Genesis 1:1 reads, *"In the beginning God created the Heavens and the earth."* In the original language, nested in between the words *"God"* and *"the heavens,"* appears the letters "את" (ALEPH TAV). "א" is the Aleph, the first letter in the Hebrew alphabet. "ת" is the "Tav," the last letter. When you place them side-by-side, these letters do not form a word. That is why they were not translated into English. Yet these letters appear paired together throughout the Old Testament just as they do here in Genesis 1:1 (see FIGURE 1: note that Hebrew is read from right to left.)

the earth: and the heavens God created the In beginning

FIGURE 1

In the original Hebrew, there are seven words that make up Genesis 1:1. What is truly amazing is that the "תא" (ALEPH TAV) letter combination shows up right in the center of the verse. There is something very significant about these two Hebrew letters. Again, they are the first and the last letters of the Hebrew alphabet!

Is it a coincidence that the Spirit of God moved on Moses as he was writing the Book of Genesis to inject the first and last letters of Hebrew right in the center of the opening line of the Bible? Absolutely not! The Aleph Tav is God's stamp that signifies Jesus. This is not the only place where the Aleph Tav stamp occurs in the Bible. It is placed all throughout the Word. There is no doubt that when you see the pattern of this happening throughout the pages of Scripture, you realize that these letters were placed there by God Himself as a "signature" pointing to the authority and power of His Son, Jesus Christ, the manifested Word of God!

As a kid I remember watching my dad sign his name. He would carefully sign his signature with perfect incursive writing that was unique to him. Early on, my signature was similar. However, as I grew into manhood and took on responsibilities, I developed my own unique signature. It may be hard for some to read my signature. Most can only make out the "J" and the "M." Those that have read my letters likely recognize my signature. My wife and kids have tried to duplicate, but can't —it's unique to me. The same is true for God's signature. A signature is used in letters, contracts, and other legal documents to bind the signer to what's been written. God has bound Himself to His Word! He has signed His approval and authority throughout His Word and His signature is very unique —I believe His signature is the Aleph Tav!

In Biblical times, as it is today, a seal would be used to prove owner-ship, authenticity, and to guarantee security. You may have seen pictures of these wax seals imprinted by the guarantor. In earlier eras, before the modern envelope, it was common practice to seal a letter with a wax stamp imprinted with the sender's family-specific signet ring. This ring would actually be used to imprint the wax seal proving the letter to be authentic. Jezebel used Ahab's seal to send out a letter pretending to be her husband. Notice 1 Kings 21:8, "*So she wrote letters in Ahab's name, and sealed them with his seal, and sent the letters unto the elders and to the nobles that were in his city, dwelling with Naboth.*" Both the order to annihilate and to bless the Jews was sealed by Ahasuerus' signet ring when he reigned. See Esther 3:12; 8:8, 10. Without exhausting this topic, I want you to see that the seal has been used to confirm authenticity, security, and ownership. There is a pattern of the "seal" both in the Old and New Testaments.

But thou, O Daniel, shut up the words, **and seal the book**, even to the time of the end: many shall run to and

fro, and knowledge shall be increased. —DANIEL 12:4
(emphasis added)

³³He that hath received his testimony hath set to his seal that God is true. ³⁴For he whom God hath sent speaketh the words of God: for God giveth not the Spirit by measure unto him. —JOHN 3:33-34 (emphasis added)

The term "seal" can be used both literally and figuratively in Scripture. Daniel was told to "seal the book." I believe that the seal that is upon God's Word can only be broken by the Holy Spirit. I don't believe it's possible to truly see the riches of the Word without the Holy Spirit opening the Word to us. Ephesians 4:30 records that believers are sealed by the Holy Spirit to confirm they belong to the Lord. Jesus taught that a "seal" solidified the words of the one who testifies. Therefore, the Testaments (Old and New) have been sealed by God—again proving ownership or to be authentic. Jesus stated in John 6:27 that He had the "seal" of the Father.

With these thoughts in mind, I believe that "את" Aleph Tav [JESUS], is the seal or signature of God upon His Word. This seal, signet, or 'signature' is found throughout His Word. It's as if God Himself imprinted his 'signet' on His Word —because He did!

THE FIRST AND THE LAST

Who hath wrought and done it, calling the generations from the beginning? I the Lord, the first, and with the last; I am he. —ISAIAH 41:4

Thus saith the Lord the King of Israel, and his redeemer the Lord of hosts; I am the first, and I am the last; and beside me there is no God. —ISAIAH 44:6

Hearken unto me, O Jacob and Israel, my called; I am he; I am the first, I also am the last. —ISAIAH 48:12

In these verses the Lord literally refers to Himself as *"the first and the last."* This is recorded in both the Old and New Testaments. Jesus said in Revelation 1:17, *"Fear not; I am the first and the last."* This is also recorded in Revelation 1:11; 2:8, 19; and 22:13. With the appearance of the first and last letters of Hebrew throughout the Bible, beginning in Genesis 1:1, we can now see what He was referring to. When Jesus says, *"I am the first and the last,"* He is literally saying, *"I am the ALEPH and the TAV!"*

When you consider Jesus' words in context, it is clear that He is referring to the letters of the alphabet. Remember, though translated in Greek, Jesus stated in Revelation 1:11, *"I am Alpha [ALEPH] and Omega [TAV], the first and the last."* Jesus is saying that He is not only the Word, but that He is the letters that make up the Word–specifically, *the first and the last*—the ALEPH TAV!

With that in mind, let's consider what appears in the center of Genesis 1:1. It is none other than the sign or signature of Jesus, the ALEPH TAV. Truly, "*In the beginning was the Word, and the Word was with God, and the Word was God*" (John 1:1). Jesus has challenged us to place emphasis on the very letters that make up His Word. "*For verily I say unto you, Till heaven and earth pass, **one jot** or **one tittle** shall in no wise pass from the law, till all be fulfilled*" (Matthew 5:18, emphasis added).

As powerful as it is to see the integrity of God's Word come to light, there is so much more to see and discover when it comes to the beauty of His Word! It is wonderful to see how God has preserved the purity of His Word. I'm in awe of the amazing details that He has laid up for us to discover. When one studies the Word, its beauty, framework, architecture, and infallibleness become absolutely clear. None other than a Holy God could have penned such words in an irrefutable structure!

Everything about the Word directs us to Jesus. God has laid out His Word to the smallest detail in order to point us to the saving knowledge of the Savior. The thoughts of a carnal man could never penetrate to the depths and integrity of the Word of God! God has not only preserved His Word, but has framed it with the architecture and blueprint of the deepest and richest language known to man!

Let us now go deeper into this study of Jesus, the Aleph Tav (the first and the last). In order to truly appreciate the wisdom of God, we need a clear understanding of the language He authored from the beginning.

Hebrew has been argued to be the oldest recorded language. This language has a unique beauty. Unlike the English alphabet, each letter of the Hebrew alphabet carries an independent, specific meaning and a numeric value. There are 22 letters in all. We are going to focus on the ALEPH and the TAV.

The ALEPH is the first letter of Hebrew. It carries a numerical value of 1 or 1,000. Hebrew was originally depicted using pictures called pictograms. In this ancient form, the ALEPH was depicted as an OX HEAD. This letter is symbolic of God, strength, and service. In Greek, it is 'Alpha' and in English, it is our 'A'. As a matter a fact, the construction of our letter 'A' is derived from the ancient pictogram of an ox head [See FIGURE 2]. The Greek word, "alphabet," is taken from the first two letters of Greek, *Alpha* and *Beta* —and it is where we get the word, "*alphabet*." This was taken from the original Hebrew language, *Aleph* "A" and *Bet* "B."

FIGURE 2

The TAV is the last letter of the Hebrew alphabet and it carries the numerical value of 400. In the Ancient Hebrew pictograms, the TAV is portrayed as a cross (two sticks crossed over one another). This letter is symbolic of a mark, covenant, or destination.

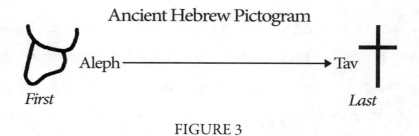

Ancient Hebrew Pictogram

Aleph ⟶ Tav

First   Last

FIGURE 3

In Hebrew each letter in the alphabet carries a meaning. When you place two letters beside one another, a message can be delivered. When you put the meanings of the ALEPH and the TAV together, something beautiful unfolds!

ALEPH–OX HEAD — symbolic of God, strength and service.

TAV–CROSS — representing a mark, covenant or destination.

So the ALEPH TAV represents a strong-covenant or serving a destination [See FIGURE 3]. It is easy to see how these letters represent Jesus. He was a servant who came to offer a strong covenant of salvation. It was sealed in His own blood when He laid down His life in love at the cross. *"Greater love hath no man than this, that a man lay down his life for his friends"* (John 15:13).

When plowing a field with an ox, the plowman drives the ox towards a mark in the distance in order to keep the rows straight. Likewise, Jesus came into this earth with the destination or mark of the cross! It was on that cross that He eternally sealed the covenant of our salvation! Jesus is *the first and the last*, He is the ALEPH TAV!

Chapter 4

BEFORE THE FOUNDATION OF THE WORLD

Who verily was foreordained before the foundation of
the world, but was manifest in these last times for you.
—1 PETER 1:20

There is something completely unique about the Bible. It was composed by roughly 40 authors, spanning roughly 1500 years, by men of diverse backgrounds and fields of work. Their writings portray perfect harmony. This validates the fact that the true author of the Bible is the Spirit of God! Only one who stands outside of time could have declared such truths and prophecies that transcend time and location. There are many things that distinguish God from all of the idols of man in the world. One thing stands out above of them all: His ability to tell the end from the beginning!

Who hath declared from the beginning, that we may know? and beforetime, that we may say, He is righteous? yea, there is none that sheweth, yea, there is none that declareth, yea, there is none that heareth your words. — ISAIAH 41:26 (emphasis added)

[9]Remember the former things of old: for I am God, and there is none else; I am God, and there is none like me, [10]**Declaring the end from the beginning, and from ancient times the things that are not yet done**, saying, My counsel shall stand, and I will do all my pleasure. — ISAIAH 46:9-10 (emphasis added)

[3]**I have declared the former things from the beginning;** and they went forth out of my mouth, and I shewed them; I did them suddenly, and they came to pass. [5]**I have even from the beginning declared it to thee**; before it came to pass I shewed it thee: lest thou shouldest say, Mine idol hath done them, and my graven image, and my molten image, hath commanded them. [6]Thou hast heard, see all this; and will not ye declare it. —ISAIAH 48:3, 5, 6A (emphasis added)

In the verses above, we see that God declares the end from the beginning. He speaks from ancient times the things that are not yet done. He declares things before they come to pass so that no man can take the credit nor offer glory to an idol made by man.

The historical novelist WILBUR SMITH once made this shrewd assessment:

> *"Mohammedanism cannot point to any prophecies of the coming of Mohammed uttered hundreds of years before his birth. Neither can the founders of any cult in this country rightly identify any ancient text specifically foretelling their appearance."*

One of the most beautiful realities of Christ is that His arrival was foretold long before His birth. Josh McDowell states in his book, *Evidence that Demands a Verdict: Volume 1*, that Jesus fulfilled 353 prophecies that were written about His life. From the very beginning, right after the sin of man, God promised to bring forth a seed from the womb of the woman that would crush the enemy (Genesis 3:15). He declared that this crushing of the enemy would bruise the heel of the Son. The enemy would receive a mortal wound while the Son would receive a temporary one. Galatians 4:4 declares, *"But when the fullness of the time was come, God sent forth his Son, made of a woman, made under the law."* Many believers miss the beauty of God's Son being manifested in the earth. They believe His very origin was in Bethlehem, not recognizing that His birth was prophesied and expected by many generations. Before the virgin named Mary, and before Bethlehem, there was the Word! The place of His birth was foretold in Micah 5:2. The time of His birth was declared in Daniel 9:25 and Genesis 49:10. The manner of His birth was described in Isaiah 7:14. Christ coming into this world to redeem us from our sin was a part of God's plan since the foundation of the world!

Our God is omniscient — all-knowing, all-wise, and all-seeing. The enemy didn't surprise God when he showed up in the Garden of Eden to lure man into sin. God wasn't taken by surprise as Adam hid himself after he had sinned. Hidden within the text of Scripture, we find that God had a plan for redemption from before the foundation of the world.

Don't allow the enemy to accuse and condemn you in your sin to the point of hopelessness. God had a plan for your salvation before you were ever born. There is nothing in this life that can thwart His plan and His will to save all who call upon Him in faith! Your history doesn't have to define your destiny! Your destiny is in the hands of a merciful God whose thoughts for you are peace and not evil, to give you an expected end (Jeremiah 29:11)! God is not moved by our mistakes of the past. He has had a plan for our salvation since before the foundation of the world! Make a decision to receive your salvation through Jesus Christ!

There are five occasions in the New Testament where we see evidence that God's plan for our salvation was established before "*the foundation of the world.*" God has laid up a message in His Word to prove that He had intended from the very beginning to save man by sending His Son Jesus. Notice the following verses (emphasis added):

That it might be fulfilled which was spoken by the prophet, saying, I will open my mouth in parables; I will utter things which have been kept secret **from the foundation of the world**. —MATTHEW 13:35

For we which have believed do enter into rest, as he said, As I have sworn in my wrath, if they shall enter into my rest: although the works were finished **from the foundation of the world**. —HEBREWS 4:3

For then must he often have suffered **since the foundation of the world**: but now once in the end of the world hath he appeared to put away sin by the sacrifice of himself. —HEBREWS 9:26

According as he hath chosen us in him **before the foundation of the world**, that we should be holy and without blame before him in love: —EPHESIANS 1:4

Who verily was foreordained **before the foundation of the world**, but was manifest in these last times for you. —1 PETER 1:20

"IN THE BEGINNING"

As we discussed earlier, in the original Hebrew alphabet each pictogram is a letter with a numeric value and a symbolic meaning. With that in mind, it's interesting to study the very first word in the Bible, '*Barasheet*'. We read that word in English as, "*In the beginning.*" Its spelling portrays a message in the original language that is absolutely amazing! As I attempt to unfold this, keep in mind that, "*In the beginning was the Word*" (John 1:1).

If we were to look up the Hebrew pictogram meaning of each letter that is used to spell "*Barasheet*," a message can be found. In Hebrew, *Barasheet* is spelled using these letters: BET, RESH, ALEPH, SHIN, YOD, TAV. Let's consider the meaning of each letter:

BET is the equivalent of our letter B, and is depicted in the ancient Hebrew pictograms as a house, tent or lineage.

RESH (R) is depicted as a man's head. It means the first or highest person.

ALEPH (A), is depicted as an ox head, meaning strength, service or God.

SHIN (S or Sh) is depicted as two teeth, meaning to consume or destroy.

YOD (Y) is depicted as a man's arm, meaning efforts or works.

TAV (T) is depicted as two crossed sticks, meaning mark, destination, or covenant.

A truly remarkable connection can be made here. Notice that the first two letters of the first word in the Bible literally mean "*first born of the house*" or "*son*." When you add the following letters you see the meanings of "*service, strength or God;*" "*consumed or destroyed;*" "*hands;*" and a "*cross*." If you took each individual letter of the first word in the Bible, taken from its original language and meaning, it would symbolize the following message: "*The SON OF GOD, CONSUMED or DESTROYED with HANDS on a CROSS!*" All of that can be discovered by studying the individual Hebrew pictograms that make up the word "*Barasheet*" or "*In the beginning.*" Interestingly, Jesus said in the New Testament,

Destroy this temple [or HOUSE], and in three days I will raise it up. —JOHN 2:19

You truly can't get any closer to "*In the beginning*" than literally laying out the plan of salvation through the original alphabet that spells "*In the beginning!*" The Bible is the living Word of God. You cannot exhaust it! One can never fully grasp all of its hidden riches of wisdom, knowledge, and glory! I get a kick out those who say, "*I've read the Bible.*" The Bible is not a book that you read like you would a novel or historic publication. One can't be given a test to see if they have learned it. The Word of God is living, and by the Spirit of God it is ever revealing more and more to those who seek its glory!

THE GENERATIONS OF ADAM

> This is the book of the generations of Adam. In the day that God created man, in the likeness of God made he him. —GENESIS 5:1

As we continue to study Jesus, the Aleph Tav (the first and the last), I want us to take a look at the first man, Adam. He was a type, or shadow, that pointed to Jesus. The New Testament calls Jesus *"the last Adam"* (1 Corinthians 15:45). There are many things in the Bible that allude to Jesus and foreshadow His life on earth. There's a theme that is established in Genesis of *"the first and the last."*

The Bible teaches that *"Adam was not deceived, but the woman being deceived was in the transgression"* (1 Timothy 2:14). This is a perfect picture of Christ and the church (His bride). We were the ones in the transgression. I believe that when Eve sinned, she immediately saw the result of that sin. She and Adam were originally clothed in glory. Once Eve disobeyed God, sin was introduced and that glory departed (Psalms 8:4, Romans 3:23). It would have caused an immediate difference in her physical appearance that Adam would have noticed. After having seen her in her new state, or condition after sin, he willingly followed her and bore the same judgment that he knew would come from disobeying God. Eve literally became a "Gentile" bride. Her sin put her outside of the covenant with God. Yet, she would be redeemed. Eve was the first. This same story is paralleled in Ruth. It was fulfilled with Christ and His Gentile Bride (the church) as the last. One could say that Adam sacrificed himself for his wife! This could easily be seen as a picture of Jesus, the last Adam, who was completely sinless, offering Himself for our sins on the cross at Calvary.

> For he hath made him to be sin for us, who knew no sin;
> that we might be made the righteousness of God in him.
> —2 CORINTHIANS 5:21

From the moment Adam sinned, God's plan of salvation and redemption began to unfold. When Adam and Eve sinned, they became fearful and hid from God. God's answer to Adam's new found fear came in the form of a sacrifice. In Genesis 3:21, God chose to shed innocent blood to cover the sin and shame of Adam and Eve, and to replace the clothing they lost. Though they lost their original covering of God's glory, God did not leave them that way. Even after they disobeyed Him, God provided a sacrifice, of what I believe to be a lamb, to clothe them. This is an obvious picture of Jesus, the Lamb of God, who would take away the sin of the world (John 1:29).

God prophesied that there would come forth a seed out of the womb of the woman that would crush the serpent (the devil) and would bruise the heel of her seed (the Son). See Genesis 3:15 and Hebrews 2:14. Galatians 4:4 applauds that prophecy as having been fulfilled in Jesus, who on the cross crushed the enemy while His heel was yet bruised!

> Who hath wrought and done it, calling the generations
> from the beginning? I the Lord, the first, and with the
> last; I am he. —ISAIAH 41:4

In this verse, God says that He calls generations from the beginning. Years ago, I was reading over the generations of Adam in Genesis 5. Through the years, I've picked up some limited knowledge of the meaning of some of the names in the Old Testament (particularly the Book of Genesis). As I was reading over the names of each successive generation, I noticed something that I want to share with you here. If you take the first 10 names listed in the generations of Adam it will take you up to Noah. If you then take the meaning of each of those ten names in succession, it literally tells a story that points to Jesus! Notice the following names and their meanings as revealed in the King James Bible:

ADAM–man

SETH–appointed

ENOS–mortal

CAINAN–sorrow

MAHALALEEL–the blessed God

JARED–shall come down

ENOCH–teaching

METHUSELAH–His death shall bring

LAMECH–the despairing

NOAH–comfort & rest

Put them all together and it reads something like this: "*Man was appointed mortal sorrow, but the blessed God shall come down teaching. His death shall bring the despairing comfort and rest!*"

The first genealogy in Scripture literally points to the message of the Bible from beginning to end! Only a God of infinite wisdom could lay up such treasures in His Word that consistently reiterate the same message, theme, and redemptive plan! Jesus is the manifested Word of God and everything in it points to Him!

THE END FROM THE BEGINNING

As I shared at the opening of this chapter, there is a pattern in Scripture of God's unique ability to declare the end from the beginning. There are so many "*firsts*" in Scripture that literally point to the "*last.*" This becomes a clear revelation that points directly to Jesus, the Aleph Tav (the first and the last). Even in the last words of the final prophecy of Scripture, we read, "*I am Alpha and Omega [ALEPH and TAV], the beginning and the end, the first and the last*" (Revelation 22:13). The end points to the beginning and the beginning points to the end — Jesus, the Aleph Tav!

There is also a numerical message to be seen. It indicates that man has around 6,000 years on this earth before we enter into the 7,000 year time frame—the Millennium and earthly reign of our soon coming King! Jesus is coming again and I believe it will be before the 7,000th year time frame. It's interesting that when you look at the first statement in the Bible, it contains a total of 6 *Alephs*. The Aleph has the numerical value of 1 or 1,000. Was God saying from the beginning that creation would take 6 days and that man would be given 6,000 years? 2 Peter 3:8 says, *"with the Lord one day is as a thousand years, and a thousand years as one day."* Oh the depths of His Word! To think that all from the beginning to the end, even time itself, was established in the very beginning!

We know now that the first Adam was a picture of Jesus, who is called the *"last Adam"* (1 Corinthians 15:45). The first sacrifice (undoubtedly a lamb) offered in Scripture pointed to Jesus, the final Lamb offered for the sin of the world (John 1:29). Abel being slain for His righteousness pointed to Christ (Hebrews 12:24). Abraham offering his son Isaac (who was spared) on the Mount in Genesis 22:1-13 is a perfect picture of Jesus being offered by His Father and then raised from the dead. Abraham literally believed that God would have raised his son Isaac from the dead (Romans 4:17; Hebrews 17:19). Abraham developed an image in his mind's eye of God raising Isaac from the dead. God took that vision and fulfilled it when He raised Jesus, His own Son, from the dead! No wonder Jesus said, *"Your father Abraham rejoiced to see my day: and he saw it, and was glad"* (John 8:56).

I am convinced that if you read the Bible looking for Jesus, the Spirit of God will begin to open up the Word to you like never before! Accounts, stories, events, celebrations, miracles, weddings, judgments, deliverances, men, women, prophets and kings throughout the Bible all point to one Man—Jesus, the Christ! Abraham and a new nation of people, Isaac's willful sacrifice, his Gentile wife (a picture of the Church) all point to Jesus. The first time the word "love" is used in the Bible is in reference to Abraham's love for his son Isaac—this is a picture of the Father's love for Jesus, the Son (Genesis 22:2). It's amazing that you don't hear of Isaac after he was laid on the altar until he is seen calling for his wife. This in itself is another picture of Jesus! The list goes on — Joseph's betrayal by his own brothers and his glorious success that took him from the pit to the palace! Moses' mass exodus of the people of God; His staff, the miracles, and even the brazen (judged) serpent he placed on a stick that brought healing (John 3:14) all pointed to Jesus! These are just a few of the countless examples that all represent Jesus.

> For Moses truly said unto the fathers, A prophet shall the Lord your God raise up unto you of your brethren, like unto me; him shall ye hear in all things whatsoever he shall say unto you. —ACTS 3:22

The "*glory*" of Moses was a type of Christ (2 Corinthians 3:7). Jesus is the fulfillment of all Law and prophecy recorded in the Old Testament. Think of it this way, Jesus = Law and Prophecy. Scripture refers to Moses as "*the one by whom came the Law.*" Elijah is referred to as "*a mighty prophet who never saw death.*" So, Moses = Law, and Elijah = Prophecy. I believe that is why God chose Moses and Elijah to appear before Him in Matthew 17 where He introduces them to His only begotten Son, Jesus! What does the Father say to these two Old Testament pillars and patriarchs? Notice Matthew 17:5, "*While he yet spake, behold, a bright cloud overshadowed them: and behold a voice out of the cloud, which said, This is my beloved Son, in whom I am well pleased; hear ye him*" (emphasis added).

Everything recorded in Scripture is fulfilled in Christ. We don't need a new word or plan for our salvation. Our salvation is a finished work! Man's words could never tap the power that's present in the Word of God! Christ is the fulfillment of our redemption and no man can add to it or take away from it. He literally looked Moses and Elijah, the two men representing the Law and prophecy, in the face and said regarding Jesus, "*hear ye him.*" It was all fulfilled in Christ. These men had once looked through a glass darkly, but now they had seen the reality of their prophecies in the face of Jesus Christ! See 2 Corinthians 4:6.

If only believers today would recognize the power and glory that is present in the Word! There is something greater than the methods of men, powerless programs, and timeless traditions. There is power in His Word! It pierces the spirit, soul and body, bringing salvation, deliverance and healing to those who will receive it!

Sadly there are many, even within the Christian faith, who have placed emphasis on things other than the Word of God. I once had a lady tell me that her pastor didn't use the Bible. She informed me that he spoke by "*word of knowledge*" and that she could not live by the limits of what's written in the Bible. Those words grieved my heart. I can't imagine building my life on any foundation other than the Word of God! We don't have to search the clouds or ask for a dream in the night. We don't have to live subject to the words of a man or a self-proclaimed prophet. All that Christ is has been laid up in His Word. He is the fulfillment of all things! Look no further than to the Ancient of Days for your salvation. He alone is the Author and Finisher of our faith!

Looking unto Jesus the author and finisher of our faith; who for the joy that was set before him endured the cross, despising the shame, and is set down at the right hand of the throne of God. —HEBREWS 12:2 (emphasis added)

I love the book of Hebrews. As you study Hebrews from chapter to chapter, you begin to pick up on a theme: the supremacy of Jesus. This book takes many characters and methods of the Old Testament and demonstrates that they are merely types and shadows that pointed to Jesus (Hebrews 10:1). The supremacy of Jesus is covered for twelve chapters in Hebrews. Chapters 1-2 denotes His supremacy over angels; Chapters 3-4, over Moses; Chapters 5-7, over the priesthood; Chapters 8-10, over the first blood covenant and testament. Lastly, chapters 11-12 speak of His supremacy over the patriarchs. Jesus is Supreme! His Word contains the power of His love, wisdom, and faith. He reigns over anything you could try to compare to Him! He is the fulfillment of all Law and Prophecy. He is the Author and Finisher of our faith and we are complete in Him who is the head of all principality and power (Colossians 2:10)!

ALEPH TAV IN THE OLD TESTAMENT

Psalm 119 offers a unique and grand portrayal of the Hebrew alphabet. It has 176 verses divided into 22 stanzas yielding 8 key words for each of the 22 letters (176 = 8 x 22). This Psalm perfectly represents the whole Hebrew alphabet in its correct order; there are no variations or missing letters. This is the longest division (chapter) in the Book of Psalms or any other book in the Bible; its theme and topic is none other than the Word of God! It literally begins with the *Aleph* and ends with the *Tav* — because Jesus is the manifested Word of God, the Aleph Tav.

The following Scriptures are just a few that I want to share; they each have the first and last letters of the Hebrew alphabet (the *Aleph* and the *Tav*) injected in them. Keep in mind that these letters do not form a word, therefore they were not translated. They only appear in the original Hebrew texts. They serve no meaning other than pointing to Jesus who has declared Himself to be *"the first and the last,"* the Aleph Tav! I would encourage you to view each verse and equate Jesus in each place where the Hebrew letters "את" (Aleph Tav) have been placed. These are only a few of the verses. There are literally hundreds that exist in the Old Testament. These Scriptures literally speak of Jesus!

In the beginning God created את the heaven and the earth. —GENESIS 1:1

And the flood was forty days upon the earth; and the waters increased, and bare up the את ark, and it was lift up above the earth. —GENESIS 7:17

And I will establish my את covenant between me and thee and thy seed after thee in their generations for an everlasting covenant, to be a God unto thee, and to thy seed after thee. —GENESIS 17:7

For I know him, that he will command his את children and his household after him, and they shall keep the way of the Lord, to do justice and judgment; that the Lord may bring upon Abraham את that which he hath spoken of him. —GENESIS 18:19

And Abraham said, My son, God will provide himself a lamb for a burnt offering: so they went both of them together. And they came to the place which God had told him of; and Abraham built an את altar there, and laid the את wood in order, and bound את Isaac his son, and laid him on the altar upon the wood. And Abraham stretched forth his את hand, and took the את knife to slay his את

son. And the angel of the Lord called unto him out of heaven, and said, Abraham, Abraham: and he said, Here am I. And he said, Lay not thine hand upon the lad, neither do thou any thing unto him: for now I know that thou fearest God, seeing thou hast not withheld thy את son, thine only את son from me. —GENESIS 22:8-12

And ye shall not swear by my name falsely, neither shalt thou profane the name of thy את God: I am the Lord. — LEVITICUS 19:12

Then will I remember my covenant את with Jacob, and also my covenant את with Isaac, and also my covenant את with Abraham will I remember; and I will remember the land. —LEVITICUS 26:42

And they kept את the passover on the fourteenth day of the first month at even in the wilderness of Sinai: according to all that the Lord commanded את Moses, so did the children of Israel. —NUMBERS 9:5

And thou shalt love את the Lord thy God with all thine heart, and with all thy soul, and with all thy might. — DEUTERONOMY 6:5

The Lord shall open unto thee his good את treasure, the את heaven to give the rain unto thy land in his season, and to bless את all the work of thine hand: and thou shalt lend unto many nations, and thou shalt not borrow. — DEUTERONOMY 28:12

And the Lord thy God will circumcise את thine heart, and את the heart of thy seed, to love the Lord thy God with all thine heart, and with all thy soul, that thou mayest live. —DEUTERONOMY 30:6

See, I have set before thee this day את life and good, and death and evil; —DEUTERONOMY 30:15

And the men said unto her, We will be blameless of this thine oath which thou hast made us swear. Behold, when we come into the land, thou shalt bind this את line of scarlet thread in the window which thou didst let us down by: and thou shalt bring thy את father, and thy את mother, and thy את brethren, and את all thy father's household, home unto thee. —JOSHUA 2:17-18

And Joshua spake unto the priests, saying, Take up את the ark of the covenant, and pass over before the people. And they took up אֵת the ark of the covenant, and went before the people. —JOSHUA 3:6

To translate the kingdom from the house of Saul, and to set up אֵת the throne of David over Israel and over Judah, from Dan even to Beersheba. —2 SAMUEL 3:10

And there came of all people to hear the אֵת wisdom of Solomon, from all kings of the earth, which had heard of his wisdom. —1 KINGS 4:34

Ye shall not need to fight in this battle: set yourselves, stand ye still, and see אֵת the salvation of the Lord with you, O Judah and Jerusalem: fear not, nor be dismayed; to morrow go out against them: for the Lord will be with you. —2 CHRONICLES 20:17

The Lord hath made bare his holy אֵת arm in the eyes of all the nations; and all the ends of the earth shall see the אֵת salvation of our God. —ISAIAH 52:10

For I am the Lord: I will speak, אֵת and the word that I shall speak shall come to pass; it shall be no more prolonged: for in your days, O rebellious house, will I say the word, and will perform it, saith the Lord God. — EZEKIEL 12:25

Neither will I hide my face any more from them: for I have poured out my את spirit upon the house of Israel, saith the Lord God. —EZEKIEL 39:29

For the earth shall be filled with the knowledge of the את glory of the Lord, as the waters cover the sea. — HABAKKUK 2:14

And I will pour upon the house of David, and upon the inhabitants of Jerusalem, the spirit of grace and of supplications: and they shall look upon me את whom they have pierced, and they shall mourn for him, as one mourneth for his only son, and shall be in bitterness for him, as one that is in bitterness for his firstborn. — ZECHARIAH 12:10

Awake, O sword, against my את shepherd, and against the man that is my fellow, saith the Lord of hosts: smite the shepherd, and the sheep shall be scattered: and I will turn mine hand upon the little ones. —ZECHARIAH 13:7

The injections of "תא" appear to be an obvious 'signature' of Jesus in order to confirm who it is that the words and prophecies speak of. There would be no other reason to insert two letters that do not form a word into the text. Considering that *the first and last* letters of Hebrew are placed side-by-side throughout the Old Testament, where messages are conveyed that point to Christ, is of major implication. The placement of the "תא" offers a direct connection to the prophecy and the fulfiller of the prophecy — the One who is called *"the first and the last"* — Jesus the Aleph Tav!

Chapter 5

ALEPH TAV: FROM GLORY TO GLORY

Ought not Christ to have suffered these things, and to
enter into his glory? —LUKE 24:26

The Bible is a love story. The plan of redemption that was laid out
from the beginning reveals the heart, mercy, grace and love of God.
One of our boys once asked me, *"Why did God create the devil?"* My reply
was along these lines: if man did not have the choice to not love God,
it would not be true love. God gives us the freedom to choose right or
wrong (Deuteronomy 30:19). We may have the choice to reject God, but
we must know that God does not reject us. In spite of ourselves and our
choices, God chooses to love us! Romans 5:8 says, *"But God commendeth
his love toward us, in that, while we were yet sinners, Christ died for us."* The
heart of God was revealed after the original sin of man. It is simple. Man
disobeyed Him and sinned. God had a choice to accept or reject man for
his disobedience. He chose love and covered man's sin. His first recorded

74

words after the fall were, *"Adam, where art thou?"* (Genesis 3:9). God's plan for redemption, prepared before man ever sinned, began to unfold. It's not that we loved Him, He first loved us (1 John 4:19). In our fallen, rebellious and sinful state, His love offers salvation!

> And without controversy great is the mystery of godliness: God was manifest in the flesh, justified in the Spirit, seen of angels, preached unto the Gentiles, believed on in the world, received up into glory. —1 TIMOTHY 3:16

Jesus was the key to God's plan for our redemption. It was a journey in which He was taken from glory to glory! The word glory represents the manifestation of who God is. The glory of something reveals its true character and attributes. Hebrews 1:3 defines it as the expressed image of who God is. Throughout the Bible, His glory shows up in different forms. The phrase, *"from glory to glory,"* reveals Him from the first to the last — the Aleph Tav. The Word of God became flesh, and we beheld His glory (John 1:1,14). The four Gospels serve as witnesses to testify of the things regarding Jesus' birth, life, passion, and victorious resurrection. The Gospels tell the story, from glory to glory!

THE FOUR GOSPELS

Each Gospel is different, yet harmonious as they each portray Christ. The fact that there are four Gospels is interesting. I have always been intrigued by the significance of numbers in the Bible and their meaning. The number four represents what God is doing in the earth as it relates to creation. Think about it, there are four points to earth's compass — north, south, east and west. There are four seasons to earth's year — spring, summer, autumn, and winter. There are four elements connected with our world — earth, air, fire, and water. In Genesis 2:10 we read of the first river that became four heads, *"And a river went out of Eden to water the garden; and from thence it was parted, and became into four heads."* There have been four, and only four, great world-empires — the Babylonian, the Medo-Persian, the Grecian, and the Roman. Scripture divides earth's inhabitants into four classes — *"kindred, and tongue, and people, and nation"* (Revelation 5:9). In the Parable of the Sower, our Lord divided the field into four kinds of soil, before He said, *"the field is the world"* (Matthew 13:4-8, 38). The fourth commandment has to do with rest from all earth's labors (Exodus 20:7-10). In 'The Lord's Prayer', the fourth clause reads, *"Thy will be done on earth"* (Matthew 6:10).

In the Book of Revelation there are four beasts who surround the throne and continually watch over the activities in the earth. The faces of these beasts show up on the veil within the Tabernacle (Exodus 26:31-34, 36:35-36). One has the face of a *lion*, one of an *ox*, one of a *man*, and one of an *eagle*. This veil in the Tabernacle represented Jesus' flesh.

> By a new and living way, which he hath consecrated
> for us, through the veil, that is to say, his flesh; —
> HEBREWS 10:20

The veil separated the Holy of Holies in the Tabernacle where God's presence dwelled. What's truly amazing is that the veil was held up by four pillars. The pillars served as a way to portray (like a portrait) the veil and the decorated emblems printed on the veil (the face of a lion, ox, man, and eagle). Its ultimate purpose was to separate the Most Holy Place from the inner and outer courts of the Tabernacle. No high priest could enter God's presence without passing through the veil. Even in the Tabernacle, Jesus is clearly seen. John 14:6, *"Jesus saith unto him, I am the way, the truth, and the life: no man cometh unto the Father, but by me."*

Notice the parallel between the Tabernacle's veil and Jesus. Both are portrayed by four pillars. The veil, called Jesus' flesh in Hebrews 10:20, was portrayed by four pillars. The life of Jesus, from birth to death and resurrection, is portrayed by four pillars — Matthew, Mark, Luke and John!

Apart from their faces, the beasts who surround the throne are identical. Likewise, the Gospels each have a *'face'* that separates them from the others. The four tribes of the twelve tribes of Israel that encamped immediately around the Tabernacle were represented by these faces as well.

The Camp of Dan to the north, the *Eagle.*

The Camp of Ephraim to the west, the *Ox.*

The Camp of Reuben to the south, the *Man.*

The Camp of Judah to the East, the *Lion.*

I truly believe that each of these faces are represented in the four Gospels. Each perspective contains symbolism related to the faces of the veil.

MATTHEW *[KING, LION, PURPLE]:* The purpose of Matthew's Gospel is made obvious from the genealogy. He is connecting Jesus to the throne as a descendant of Abraham. Matthew represents the color purple, signifying royalty. Here Jesus is portrayed as King, therefore, the face of a LION.

MARK *[SERVANT, OX, SCARLET]:* Mark's Gospel is written to show that Jesus came to serve. Servants don't need genealogies; therefore in his Gospel, it is omitted. Mark's color is scarlet, a color that represents the earth. Mark, portraying Jesus as a servant, the face of the OX.

LUKE *[SON OF MAN, FACE OF A MAN, WHITE]:* Luke is writing to prove that Jesus, though the Son of God, was indeed a man. His Gospel is represented by the face of the MAN. His color is white, symbolic of Jesus' purity, righteousness, and sinless life.

JOHN *[SON OF GOD, EAGLE, BLUE]:* John is writing to prove that Jesus is one with the Father, therefore there is no genealogy. John sums it up like this, "In the beginning was the Word, and the Word was with God, and the Word was God" (John 1:1). John is represented by the face of the EAGLE and his color is blue, the color of Heaven.

The men that the Spirit of God chose to pen these Gospels were particularly suited to the task. Each of their natural lives fit the Gospels they were to write. Matthew, writing to portray Jesus as KING, was a tax-collector that worked for the Roman Kingdom. Mark was not an Apostle but was known as the *"servant"* (2 Timothy 4:11). Luke was a physician (Colossians 4:14) and wrote to prove that Jesus was a man. John was known as the *"beloved disciple"* and was even allowed to receive the ultimate revelation of Jesus as the Son of God when He was given the prophecy recorded in the Book of Revelation.

And there are also many other things which Jesus did, the which, if they should be written every one, I suppose that even the world itself could not contain the books that should be written. Amen. —JOHN 21:25

The more you study the architecture behind the words of the Bible, the more you realize it is truly the Word of God! It is not a book written by one man proclaiming to have heard from God. The types, shadows, structure, and integrity of the text all point to a God who stands outside of time and possesses infinite wisdom!

You can trust the Word of God. Make a decision to live by it. Take God at His Word and you will see that this God is true, this God is alive! This God loves you and me so much that He sent His Son to die for our sins. He laid out His infallible Word in a unique and glorious fashion so that we would have no reason to doubt and every reason to place our faith in Jesus! Truly, *"faith cometh by hearing, and hearing by the word of God"* (Romans 10:17).

FROM GLORY TO GLORY

Tell ye, and bring them near; yea, let them take counsel together: who hath declared this from ancient time? who hath told it from that time? have not I the Lord? and there is no God else beside me; a just God and a Saviour; there is none beside me. Look unto me, and be ye saved, all the ends of the earth: for I am God, and there is none else. I have sworn by myself, the word is gone out of my mouth in righteousness, and shall not return, That unto me every knee shall bow, every tongue shall swear. — ISAIAH 45:21-23

I can hear the heart of God crying out for the lost to turn to Him and be saved. The verses from Isaiah 45 truly express God's heart. All throughout the Bible, God is beckoning us to seek Him in His Word. Sadly, many today are moving away from His Word. It is His Word that preserves the beauty, glory and power of salvation. It's easy to doubt men. It should be impossible to doubt God when you realize the integrity of the Word He has given!

The story of what Jesus has done for us is the most powerful and celebrated message of all time. That message may be debated by some, but statistically it would be hard to argue with. The Bible has more copies in print than any other book in publication. It would be difficult to find anyone who is celebrated more than Jesus Christ, the Son of God! Jesus has received adoration by men of every walk of life and in every generation since His ascension to the Father. His name is higher than any name, more powerful than any name, and more majestic than any name! There is no one who can compare to Jesus, the manifested Word of God!

THE INCARNATION

If there was one text that best reveals the story of Christ from birth to glory, I believe it is Philippians 2:5-11. These verses literally take us "*From glory to glory*" as we hear of the incarnation, humiliation, exaltation, and adoration of Jesus!

⁵Let this mind be in you, which was also in Christ Jesus:
⁶Who, being in the form of God, thought it not robbery
to be equal with God: ⁷But made himself of no reputation,
and took upon him the form of a servant, and was made
in the likeness of men: ⁸And being found in fashion as
a man, he humbled himself, and became obedient unto
death, even the death of the cross. ⁹Wherefore God also
hath highly exalted him, and given him a name which is
above every name: ¹⁰That at the name of Jesus every knee
should bow, of things in heaven, and things in earth, and
things under the earth; ¹¹And that every tongue should
confess that Jesus Christ is Lord, to the glory of God the
Father. —PHILIPPIANS 2:5-11

Merriam Webster defines 'incarnate' as having a human body, to be
invested with, or given a bodily form and human nature, to be made manifest or comprehensible. (Merriam-Webster.com). The thing (Word) itself
already existed; it is simply put into a bodily form. Consider verse 6. It
says that Jesus came in the *form* of God. This word '*form*' comes from the
Greek word, *morphe (mor-fay')*. It is the part of a man that does not change
— the *nature*. Inwardly, He was God. Jesus being born in human flesh did
not take away from Him being the Son of God. He was the Word made
flesh (John 1:14). He was taken from His original form — that of the
Word — and made incarnate as God deposited Him into a bodily form.

You will notice in Verse 7, that He was found in *"fashion as a man."* The word *'fashion'* is taken from the Greek word, *schema (skhay'-mah)*, meaning the external condition. Outwardly He was a man. Verses 6-7 speak of His *"Incarnation."*

For in him dwelleth all the fulness of the Godhead bodily. —COLOSSIANS 2:9

Behold, a virgin shall be with child, and shall bring forth a son, and they shall call his name Emmanuel, which being interpreted is, God with us. —MATTHEW 1:23

But when the fulness of the time was come, God sent forth his Son, made of a woman, made under the law. — GALATIANS 4:4

For unto us **a child is born**, unto us **a son is given**: and the government shall be upon his shoulder: and his name shall be called Wonderful, Counsellor, The mighty God, The everlasting Father, The Prince of Peace. —ISAIAH 9:6 (emphasis added)

Behold, a virgin shall be with child, and shall bring forth a son, and they shall call his name Emmanuel, which being interpreted is, **God with us.** —MATTHEW 1:23 (emphasis added)

In Isaiah 9:6, you will notice the wording, *"a child is born"* and *"a son is given."* I believe it is because the Son has always been. He existed *"in the beginning"* as the Word. His body, *"the child"* was born. The *"son"* was *"given."* The Gospels tell of His incarnation. Matthew 1:23 (above) fulfills a prophecy given by Isaiah over 700 years before Jesus' birth! (See Isaiah 7:14). He was God, wrapped in human flesh. Man doesn't go to space without a space-suit. God didn't come to the earth without an earth-suit! Jesus is called the *"image of the invisible God"* (Colossians 1:14-17). The invisible God became visible in human flesh!

He was as much God though He were never a man; yet, as much a man as though He were never God. As a babe, He was carried; but as God, He healed the lame. As a man, He hungered; but as God, He fed thousands. As a man, He wept at Lazarus' grave; but as God, He was raised from the dead. As a man, He was beaten, bruised, and wounded; but as God, He heals all infirmity. As a man, He was offered as a lamb; but as God, He is the Chief Shepherd. As a man, He was sold out for 30 pieces of silver; yet as God, His blood redeems the world. As a man, He thirsted; as God, He is the water of life. As a man, He died; but as the Son of God, He was raised with all power!

Hebrews 4:15 makes the case that Jesus was tempted as we are, yet without sin; and that He understands our infirmities. Oh what a Savior! When we call upon Him, He understands. He's not some unapproachable and untouchable God. He is a loving God that loved us so much that He wrapped Himself in human flesh and came into this world so that by His life we could overcome! He can empathize with our feelings because of His time spent in the flesh.

THE HUMILIATION

I think that many have this "super hero" mindset when it comes to Jesus' life. We view Him as this guy that would have been the most popular in school and the one that everybody wanted to hang out with. However, they fail to think of the humiliation He endured. This humiliation is portrayed in the Gospels. We read that His own considered him an outcast. They made statement's like, "*Can there any good thing come out of Nazareth?*" (John 1:46). We read in John 1:11, "*He came unto his own, and his own received him not.*" Have you ever felt rejected? Jesus knows the feeling. He is well acquainted with our pains and sorrows. He endured great humiliation on our behalf.

> [1]Who hath believed our report? and to whom is the arm of the Lord revealed? [2]For he shall grow up before him as a tender plant, and as a root out of a dry ground: he hath no form nor comeliness; and when we shall see him, there is no beauty that we should desire him. [3]He is despised and rejected of men; a man of sorrows, and acquainted with grief: and we hid as it were our faces

from him; he was despised, and we esteemed him not. ⁴Surely he hath borne our griefs, and carried our sorrows: yet we did esteem him stricken, smitten of God, and afflicted. ⁵But he was wounded for our transgressions, he was bruised for our iniquities: the chastisement of our peace was upon him; and with his stripes we are healed.

—ISAIAH 53:1-5

I must admit, I grew up with the mind-set that Jesus was the best looking, most amazing man ever. I had these visions of Him being perfect in His appearance and absolutely flawless. Yet we read above, *"there is no beauty we desire him."* The prophet Isaiah doesn't depict Him as I would have imagined. Make no mistake; He is the spotless, perfect, and sinless Son of God. However, as a man, He faced humiliation and rejection. John 7:5 shares, *"For neither did his brethren believe in him."* Jesus knew rejection His entire life. He was betrayed by one of His own disciples with a kiss (Luke 22:48). His cousin John the Baptist, the one who introduced Him, got offended at Him. After being imprisoned, John sent his disciples to ask Jesus if He was the One [the Messiah] or if they should look for another (Luke 7:20-23). The day He stood in the Synagogue and proclaimed that He was the Christ, they rejected Him saying, *"Is not this Joseph's son?"* (Luke 4:22). They even tried to throw Him over a cliff!

And all they in the synagogue, when they heard these things, were filled with wrath, And rose up, and thrust him out of the city, and led him unto the brow of the hill whereon their city was built, that they might cast him down headlong. —LUKE 4:28-29

When He was taken into judgment, He was mocked and spit upon. They mocked Him as a King when they arrayed Him in purple and put a crown of thorns on His head. *"Hail, King of the Jews!"* they shouted (John 19:3). They mocked Him as a prophet when they blind-folded Him, smote Him in the face and said, *"Prophesy, who is it that smote thee?"* (Luke 22:64). They mocked Him as a priest when they said, *"He saved others; himself he cannot save"* (Matthew 27:42, Mark 15:13, Luke 23:35). Even one of the thieves being crucified right next to Him mocked Him. They crucified Him naked, bearing our shame. They drove nails through His hands and feet. The spotless Lamb was heaven sent but earth rejected. Can you see Him suspended between heaven and earth, hanging on that tree?

[7]He was oppressed, and he was afflicted, yet he opened not his mouth: he is brought as a lamb to the slaughter, and as a sheep before her shearers is dumb, so he openeth not his mouth. [8]He was taken from prison and from judg-ment: and who shall declare his generation? for he was cut off out of the land of the living: for the transgression of my people was he stricken. [9]And he made his grave with the wicked, and with the rich in his death; because he had

done no violence, neither was any deceit in his mouth. — ISAIAH 53:7-9

Truly Jesus is the Aleph Tav. In the Hebrew language, the *Aleph* is always silent. True to the very alphabet that represents Him, Jesus remained silent. The Word says, "*he opened not his mouth*" (v.7). This faithful servant was steadfast in His assignment. Remember, the Aleph is symbolic of *God, strength,* and *service* and is depicted in the ancient pictograms as the head of an ox. This faithful Ox came to serve the cross — the *Tav* (mark, destination, or covenant)! In every facet of His life, He is seen faithfully serving! Even on the cross, Jesus was found serving His mother as He secured her care with the beloved John. "*When Jesus therefore saw his mother, and the disciple standing by, whom he loved, he saith unto his mother, Woman, behold thy son! Then saith he to the disciple, Behold thy mother! And from that hour that disciple took her unto his own home*" (John 19:26-27). Only a faithful man, consumed with His assignment, is thinking about the welfare of His mother while hanging on a cross in excruciating pain. What is holding you back from caring for those you love? In every case, in every setting, and in every way, this faithful Servant was found ministering to those in need. Matthew 20:28 declares, "*Even as the Son of man came not to be ministered unto, but to minister, and to give his life a ransom for many.*" The story of His passion is a perfect picture of *Aleph Tav* — *God's strong covenant; God serving a destination.* The *Aleph* depicts His strength and service; the *Tav* depicts the cross. Jesus is the *Aleph Tav!*

What was it that drove this faithful servant to lay down His life? What led Him to serve all those that came to Him? What ultimately led Him to the cross? From His birth, it is evident that He came to die. The manger itself serves as a sign that He is the Lamb of God, slain for our sin. The Bible tells us that it was for the joy set before Him that Jesus was willing to faithfully serve and to offer His life on the cross. What kind of joy is it to be beaten with a cat of nine tails? It could not have been joyful to have potentially 39 lashes across His back with a whip so intense it required more than one soldier to bear the series of lashings. This is a whip that had many leather straps entangled with horrific debris that would tear away the flesh of its victim. This lashing came after He had already been beaten with a reed. A reed is a long slender rod that literally bruised the skin with every lash. We were the joy set before Him. It was for us that He was willing to endure having His beard pulled out and His body stripped naked to be crucified in one of the most inhumane and cruel executions ever invented. I can assure you that it wasn't the nails that kept Him on that cross!

No man took His life. He gave His life for us! You and I were the joy that was set before Him! What would lead a man to put his life in harm's way? What would lead a man to run into a burning building? The welfare of those he loves. We are willing to put our own lives on the line to save those we truly love. Jesus freely gave Himself. At any time He could have called on legions of angels who would have moved at His command! The Aleph came to serve the Tav! He would endure the affliction and even death itself for the sake of the world — for the salvation of man — for your salvation and mine! We were the joy set before Him!

> Looking unto Jesus the author and finisher of our faith; **who for the joy that was set before him endured the cross**, despising the shame, and is set down at the right hand of the throne of God. —HEBREWS 12:2 (emphasis added)

TETELESTAI

The theme and pattern of Jesus as the first and the last, the Aleph Tav, continues on the cross. There is only one chapter in the entire Bible that is fully dedicated to describing the Passion of Christ. David, by the Spirit of God, prophesied of the cross in Psalms 22. It is amazing to see that Jesus' first utterance from the cross is recorded in the first verse of Psalms 22. It is no coincidence that His last utterance on the cross is also the last verse taken from Psalms 22. Jesus quotes the first and last verses! Again, *He is the first and the last — the Aleph Tav!*

If you study the events of the crucifixion in each of the four Gospels, you will discover the first and last statements made by Jesus on the cross (see Matthew 27:32-54; Mark 15:22-39; Luke 23:33-49; John 19:16-37). There were a total of seven sayings of Jesus on the cross, but it is the first and last that I want us to pay attention to. If you look at the chronological order of each saying in light of each of the four Gospels, it is easy to establish the first and the last. They are as follows: First, *"My God, my God, why hast thou forsaken me?"* (See Matthew 27:46). Last, *"It is finished"* (see John 19:30).

The first and last sayings of Jesus continue to support His identity as the Aleph Tav. You can't truly appreciate and honor the awesome nature of His Word until you have studied it line upon line, and precept upon precept (Isaiah 28:9-10). Jesus is the manifested Word of God and He left nothing undone. He is the faithful Ox that came to fulfill His destination — the Covenant of our salvation!

The 23rd Psalm is probably the most quoted passage of Scripture in the entire Bible. However, it is the previous chapter that demonstrates the price that was paid so that we might say, *"The Lord is my Shepherd; I shall not want; And Though I walk through the valley of the shadow of death, I will fear no evil."* And let's not forget the promise of "I will dwell in the house of the Lord forever." These faith building Scriptures are preceded by a record of the crucifixion.

The following verses from Psalm 22 portray Jesus on the cross: *"For dogs have compassed me: the assembly of the wicked have inclosed me: **they pierced my hands and my feet**"* (verse 16, emphasis added); *"They part my garments among them, and cast lots upon my vesture"* (verse 18). You might ask, *"What does this have to do with the first and last sayings of Jesus on the cross?"* Let me further explain.

You may have heard the term, *"from A to Z."* It implies the entire alphabet without actually having to cite all the letters in between. In the

91

same way Jesus gave us the first and last statements of Psalm 22 on the cross; thus implying that He is the Aleph (first) and the Tav (last). Psalms 40:7 and Hebrews 10:7 teach us that Jesus came in the volume of the book (the Word of God). It is awesome to see that the 22nd Psalms opens with, *"My God, my God, why hast thou forsaken me?"* and closes with, *"It is Finished!"* (Amplified Bible).

> My God, my God, why hast thou forsaken me? why art thou so far from helping me, and from the words of my roaring? —PSALMS 22:1

> They shall come and shall declare His righteousness to a people yet to be born — that He has done it [that it is finished]! —PSALMS 22:31 [Amplified Bible]

"It is finished," is translated from a single word, *'tetelestai'*. This word describes a debt that has been paid. It means closure or ending. This word represents a battle that has been won, a debt that has been paid, and a Book or prophecy that is complete! Salvation is a finished work! Healing is a finished work! Our deliverance is a finished work! Success in our family and finances is a finished work! Forgiveness from sin is a finished work! Eternal life and redemption are finished works!

> Therefore doth my Father love me, because I lay down my life, that I might take it again. No man taketh it from me,

but I lay it down of myself. I have power to lay it down, and I have power to take it again. This commandment have I received of my Father. —JOHN 10:17-18

Jesus answered, Thou couldest have no power at all against me, except it were given thee from above: therefore he that delivered me unto thee hath the greater sin. —JOHN 19:11

32The place of the scripture which he read was this, He was led as a sheep to the slaughter; and like a lamb dumb before his shearer, so opened he not his mouth: 33In his humiliation his judgment was taken away: and who shall declare his generation? for his life is taken from the earth. 34And the eunuch answered Philip, and said, I pray thee, of whom speaketh the prophet this? of himself, or of some other man? —ACTS 8:32-34

Notice verse 33 in the Amplified Bible, "Justice was removed, denied and caused to cease!"

For he hath made him to be sin for us, who knew no sin; that we might be made the righteousness of God in him. —2 CORINTHIANS 2:21

THE EXALTATION

"This Jesus of Nazareth, without money and arms, conquered more millions than Alexander, Caesar, Mohammed, and Napoleon; without science and learning, He shed more light on things human and divine than all philosophers and scholars combined; without the eloquence of schools, He spoke such words of life as were never spoken before or since, and produced effects which lie beyond the reach of orator or poet; without writing a single line, He set more pens in motion, and furnished themes for more sermons, orations, discussions, learned volumes, works of art, and songs of praise than the whole army of great men of ancient and modern times." —PHILIP SCHAFF, The Person of Christ, American Tract Society, 1913

Because of all that He endured, God has exalted Him. Jesus finished the work that He had been given of His Father and has now been exalted! The first recorded words of Jesus in the Bible were, "*And he said unto them, How is it that ye sought me? wist ye not that I must be about my Father's business?*" (Luke 2:49). His last words before His death on the cross were "*It is finished*" (John 19:30). He is the Aleph Tav and He has been exalted!

There's no other name like the Name of Jesus! God has exalted Him and given Him a name above every name (Philippians 2:9)! The Book of Revelation declares that He is "*KING OF KINGS AND LORD OF*

LORDS" (Revelation 19:16). The Lamb of the Gospels has become the Lion of Revelation. The victim is now the Victor! His crown of thorns has been replaced with the Royal Diadem! He rode into Jerusalem on a donkey, but He's coming again on a white stallion! He is exalted! His Name offers power, dominion, and is filled with glory. His Name brings salvation, deliverance, healing, peace, power, and praise! His Name is uttered in the prayers of nations and declared in the songs of every generation. Acts 4:12 declares, *"Neither is there salvation in any other: for there is none other name under heaven given among men, whereby we must be saved." "For whosoever shall call upon the name of the Lord shall be saved"* (Romans 10:13).

THE ADORATION

His cross of suffering has become our emblem of worship! His words have become our anthems of praise! I love what the famous essay, "One Solitary Life," says of Jesus:

> He was born in an obscure village, the child of a peasant woman. He grew up in another obscure village, where He worked in a carpenter shop until He was thirty. Then for three years He was an itinerant preacher. He never had a family or owned a home. He never set foot inside a big city. He never traveled two hundred miles from the place He was born. He never wrote a book, or held an office.

He did none of the things that usually accompany greatness. While He was still a young man, the tide of popular opinion turned against Him. His friends deserted Him. He was turned over to His enemies, and went through the mockery of a trial. He was nailed to a cross between two thieves. While He was dying, His executioners gambled for the only piece of property He had —His coat. When He was dead, He was taken down and laid in a borrowed grave.

Nineteen centuries have come and gone, and today He is the central figure for much of the human race. All the armies that ever marched, and all the navies that ever sailed, and all the parliaments that ever sat, and all the kings that ever reigned, put together, have not affected the life of man upon this earth as powerfully as this One Solitary Life. —This essay was adapted from a sermon by DR. JAMES ALLAN FRANCIS in "The Real Jesus and Other Sermons" ©1926 by the Judson Press of Philadelphia

Jesus is adored by many. To *adore* means to worship; to express reverence and homage. Adoration comes in many forms. The Jews expressed adoration by putting off their shoes (Exodus 3:5; Joshua. 5:15), and by prostration (Genesis 17:3; Psalms 95:6; Isaiah 44:15, 17, 19; 46:6). To "*kiss the Son*" in Psalms 2:12 is to adore and worship him. (See Daniel 3:5-6.)

A major form of adoration is worship and spiritual songs. I believe there is a divine order of thanksgiving, praise and worship. We enter into His gates with thanksgiving, and into His courts with praise (Psalms 100:4). We worship Him in the beauty of holiness (Psalms 96:9). Thanksgiving, praise, and worship appear as progression when you compare these verses to the layout of the Tabernacle. You enter His "*gates*" with *thanksgiving* (the outer court). You enter His "*courts*" with *praise* (the inner court); and *worship* Him in the beauty of "*holiness*" (the Holy Place). Thanksgiving, praise, and worship are major components of adoration.

> And be not drunk with wine, wherein is excess; but be filled with the Spirit; Speaking to yourselves in psalms and hymns and spiritual songs, singing and making melody in your heart to the Lord. —EPHESIANS 5:18-19

According to Statista.com, over 128 million Christian / Gospel albums were sold from 2008 through 2012. There are over 140 contemporary songs about the blood; over 325 about the cross; over 100 about the resurrection; and over 200 about His sacrifice and the Lamb [Source: worshiptogether.com]. It has been over 2,000 years since Jesus gave His life on Calvary's tree and people are still singing about it! The modern list of songs about Jesus compared to those sang over the last 2,000 years is like comparing a drop of water to a swimming pool! The earliest songs of the Christian church, known as the Gregorian Chant, were written in 450 AD by Pope Gregory. More songs were written in the second and third century church from the Psalms of David (Old Testament). The earliest performers and writers of music were the church.

I was visiting with our worship pastor, Jeremiah Woods, on this topic when he stated, "*Some people think the breadth of music is only what they are exposed to from day to day. It's almost like how we are one of billions of stars in a galaxy, of billions of galaxies. Jesus has been glorified in song since before He even arrived on the earth! He is and will always be the Author of music, and His Name has been praised throughout the generations.*" His birth was marked by adoration (Luke 2:13-14) as was His resurrection. The Risen Savior is adored in heaven after His triumphant resurrection (Revelation 5:9-14).

I would challenge anyone to find one single person, throughout all ages who is as influential as Jesus Christ! Undoubtedly, He is worshipped, followed, proclaimed, loved, and *adored* more than any person or thing in human history! To gain global popularity in any generation is a huge feat; but to maintain global popularity, worship and adoration for over 2,000 years is an accomplishment on an epic and supernatural scale!

One of my favorite hymns is one we are accustomed to singing around Christmas, "O Come All Ye Faithful." I particularly love the stanza:

"All Hail! Lord, we greet Thee,

Born this happy morning,

O Jesus! for evermore be Thy name adored.

Word of the Father, now in flesh appearing;

O come, let us adore Him,

O come, let us adore Him,

O come, let us adore Him,

Christ the Lord."

—JOHN F. WADE, 18th Century

The lyrics, "*Word of the Father, now in flesh appearing*" moves me to tears whenever I sing this hymn. That is who Jesus is — the manifested Word of God! O come, let us adore Him! When you see Him through the lens of His Word, you can't help but to adore Him! I am convinced that to know Him is to love and worship Him! I implore you, find a Bible-based church where it is truly all about Jesus and His Word. Find a place where He is worshiped and you are challenged to live a surrendered life to the One who alone is worthy of adoration.

Chapter 6

THE TREE OF LIFE, THE ALMOND ROD AND THE CROSS

There are many lines that are woven throughout Scripture that lead us to the Cross. In my opinion, one of the most beautiful revelations of Jesus, the Aleph Tav, is the pattern of events that prove that Jesus existed from the beginning as the Word. The plan for our salvation was established before the foundation of the world. I do not believe I could begin to scratch the surface in this book of all the ways God has conveyed His plan. The Old Testament is packed with revelation of Jesus! I once heard it said, "*The Old Testament is Jesus concealed. The New Testament is Jesus revealed!*" I will attempt to portray a small glimpse in the pages ahead.

THE TREE OF LIFE

From the beginning, in the Book of Genesis, the "Tree of Life" is established as an emblem of eternal life with God. I believe Scripture supports a line drawn from the Tree of Life to the Cross of Calvary. Jesus came to fulfill an eternal plan to offer life — and it was given on a tree! The Tree of Life is seen in the Garden of Eden as well as in the new Jerusalem in Revelation 22:3. Therefore, it's at the beginning of the Bible and the end.

> So he drove out the man; and he placed at the east of the garden of Eden Cherubims, and a flaming sword which turned every way, to keep the way of the tree of life. — GENESIS 3:24

> [1]And he shewed me a pure river of water of life, clear as crystal, proceeding out of the throne of God and of the Lamb. [2]In the midst of the street of it, and on either side of the river, was there the tree of life, which bare twelve manner of fruits, and yielded her fruit every month: and the leaves of the tree were for the healing of the nations. [3]And there shall be no more curse: but the throne of God and of the Lamb shall be in it; and his servants shall serve him: —REVELATION 22:1-3

After the sin of man, we see a "way" made, or a path forged, to the Tree of Life. It is a type of Tabernacle set up in the Garden of Eden where Adam and Eve would come to honor God. This path began when the Lord offered an innocent animal to cover their sin (Genesis 3:21). In doing so, He set a precedent that determined the price that must be paid in order to cover the sin of man. That price was innocent blood. *"For the life of the flesh is in the blood: and I have given it to you upon the altar to make an atonement for your souls: for it is the blood that maketh an atonement for the soul"* (Leviticus 17:11). The precedent continues when, immediately following, Abel is seen bringing a lamb to God as a sacrifice. God accepted his offer. Abel was accepted. Cain, on the other hand, brought fruit, and was not accepted. See Genesis 4:3-7. Notice that Abel, son of Adam and Eve, had heard what type of sacrifice God would accept, and by faith, brought it to Him. Cain brought the product of His own work. This is the first picture alluding to the fact that we are saved by grace through faith, and not of works (Ephesians 2:8-9).

> [4]And Abel, he also brought of the firstlings of his flock and of the fat thereof. And the LORD had respect unto Abel and to his offering: [5]But unto Cain and to his offering he had not respect. And Cain was very wroth, and his countenance fell. [6]And the LORD said unto Cain, Why art thou wroth? and why is thy countenance fallen? [7]If thou doest well, shalt thou not be accepted? and if thou doest not well, sin lieth at the door. And unto thee shall be his desire, and thou shalt rule over him. —GENESIS 4:4-7

I believe that Abel's offering was based on the faith that he received from his parents recounting the sacrifice the Lord God made for their sin in Genesis 3:21. It is important to see that Abel's sacrifice was one of faith. Hebrews 11:4 declares, *"By faith Abel offered unto God a more excellent sacrifice than Cain..."* Faith comes by hearing (Romans 10:17). Abel had surely heard about the sacrifice that was made after his parent's sin. People ask me, *"How do you know it was a lamb?"* My answer is this: The Bible is a book of patterns. Identifying them is a beautiful method of study. In doing so, Scripture reveals itself. See Isaiah 28:9-10. Once you identify a clear pattern, it will tell you what's next and also what was before. Allow me to illustrate. Consider the following numbers and find the pattern: [4] [6] [8] [10] [12] Based on the the pattern what number would you guess comes next? If you guessed 14, you would be correct. In the same way, we can identify that the number 2 would come first. I'm not saying that all patterns are that easily seen, but they are there. And there is certainly a pattern when it comes to the Lamb.

In GENESIS 4, A *lamb* was offered by Abel as a sacrifice and God accepted it.

In GENESIS 22, God provided a *lamb* in the place of Isaac.

In EXODUS 12, the *lamb* provided a "passover" for each family in Israel during the final plague of Egypt.

In LEVITICUS 16, the *lamb* provided atonement for the nation of Israel on the "Day of Atonement."

In JOHN 1:29, we read, "The next day John seeth Jesus coming unto him, and saith, Behold the *Lamb of God*, which taketh away the sin of the world."

In REVELATION 5:6, we read, "And I beheld, and, lo, in the midst of the throne and of the four beasts, and in the midst of the elders, stood a *Lamb* as it had been slain, having seven horns and seven eyes, which are the seven Spirits of God sent forth into all the earth."

In REVELATION 22:1, we read, "And he shewed me a pure river of water of life, clear as crystal, proceeding out of the throne of God and of the *Lamb*."

From Genesis 4 to Revelation 5, we see the pattern of the Lamb being the means to deliverance, redemption, and salvation. There is no reason to believe that the first sacrifice offered by God in the Garden was anything other than a lamb! There is something truly beautiful I must point out. From Genesis 4 all the way to the Gospels, every lamb was offered by man. But the first lamb in Genesis 3 was offered by God. True to His Name, He is the First and the Last, the Aleph Tav. God offered the first lamb for man and He offered the last Lamb for man — Jesus, the first and the last, the Aleph Tav!

There is something else of interest here. According to Old Testament Law, the Passover lamb had to be offered by the High Priest. Jesus came as the final Passover Lamb and true to Scriptural pattern, was offered up by the High Priest. Jesus was literally taken to Caiaphas (the High Priest), questioned, and then led to the hall of judgment (John 18:13-29). It was the High Priest who turned Jesus over to be condemned (v.28). True to the order of the Old Testament, the lamb had to be inspected by the priest before it could be offered! It's no coincidence that Jesus was in Jerusalem for four days before He was crucified being questioned and challenged by the priests. The Passover Lamb had to be in possession (to be inspected) for four days before it could be offered! Every little detail of the crucifixion fulfills Old Testament Law and Prophecy!

When you consider Cain and Abel's offerings, it appears that they were offering a sacrifice as a means of entry or "acceptance" to the Way of the Tree of Life. There are several parallels between the Garden and the Tabernacle. God set a path of entry to both, and it was the only way in. Consider the similarities. In the Garden, this path's door was on the east side. The Tabernacle entrance was on the east side. Both had only one route of entrance. It appears by Abel's offering that the only way to be accepted was by the blood of a lamb. The presence of cherubim is seen in both the Garden and the Tabernacle.

> 23Therefore the LORD God sent him forth from the garden of Eden, to till the ground from whence he was taken. 24So he drove out the man; and he placed at the east of the garden of Eden Cherubims, and a flaming sword which turned every way, to keep the way of the tree of life.
> —GENESIS 3:23-24

We also find parallels between the Tabernacle and Jesus. There are a total of seven objects that furnished the Tabernacle. The Outer Court of the Tabernacle held the Brazen Altar and the Brazen Laver. In the Inner

Court were the Golden Table of Shewbread, the Golden Candlestick (with seven branches), and the Altar of Incense. Lastly, in the Holy Place or Most Inner Court was the Mercy Seat and the Ark of the Covenant — which had two Golden Cherubim (hovering over the Mercy Seat). It was in the Most Inner Court where the blood of the lamb was brought and sprinkled upon the Mercy Seat seven times (Leviticus 16:14). Likewise, Jesus bled in seven places (His hands, feet, back, head, and side).

In Genesis 28, Jacob came across an area that he called "*Bethel*" which means "*House of God.*" It derives from *"Bet,"* which means *house* and *"El"* which means *God.* It is important to note that originally this ground was known as *"Luz,"* which means "*almonds.*" This is the place where God met with Jacob and gave him an amazing dream. The dream was confirming the Covenant that He had made with his father Isaac and grandfather Abraham. When this happened, Jacob immediately knew that He was in a sanctified place.

> [17]And he was afraid, and said, How dreadful is this place! this is none other but the house of God, and this is the gate of heaven.
> [19]And he called the name of that place Bethel: but the name of that city was called Luz at the first. — GENESIS 28:17, 19

This location has huge prophetic meaning. It is the same place where Adam and Eve were created and where the first sacrifice for sin was offered.

It is the same place that Abraham offered Isaac as a figure of the Father (God) offering His Son (Jesus). It is the place of Jacob's dream. It is the site of the Temples and the place where Jesus was crucified, buried and raised! By searching and studying the Scriptures, you see a line that began in Genesis which continued forward leading us to the Cross. God is serving (Aleph) the destination (Tav).

THE ALMOND ROD

A strong Scriptural argument can be made that Luz was the location of the original Garden of Eden. The name "*Luz*" is very interesting. It means "almonds." The Garden was named after almonds. Could it be that the Tree of Life was an almond tree? Allow me to present you with some evidence.

Here are some facts about the almond. Its name means "*in a hurry.*" The almond tree was the first to bud — therefore you can literally say it was the "*first fruit.*" The first fruit in Scripture was counted "*holy*" (Romans 11:16). In Jeremiah 1:11-2, God even compares His Word to the rod of an *almond tree!*

> And it came to pass, that on the morrow Moses went into the tabernacle of witness; and, behold, the rod of Aaron for the house of Levi was budded, and brought forth buds, and bloomed blossoms, and yielded **almonds**. — NUMBERS 17:8 (emphasis added)

In the Old Testament a situation arose over who would be the one to speak on behalf of God. It caused division between the children of Israel, so God had each candidate inscribe their name on a rod and lay it before the Ark of the Covenant. God declared that the rod that would bud (come to life) would confirm whom He would use. The next morning Moses went into the Tabernacle and Aaron's rod, representing the house of Levi, had budded (Numbers 17:8). It is amazing that it yielded none other than "*almonds!*"

Think about it. This branch had been disconnected from the tree, its source. What kind of rod or branch has life in it after it has been broken off of the tree? A rod taken from the Tree of Life might! Either way, this rod is yielding the same fruit that God has sanctified in His Word! There is an amazing connection between *the almond*, the *Tree of Life* and the *Tabernacle* — particularly, the *Seven Branched Candlestick.*

Exodus 25:31 offers the details that pertain to the Candlestick of the Tabernacle. Before I describe the Candlestick, it is important to understand the almond tree has three phases of maturity. Those three phases were a major part of the decorations, or ornaments, on the Candlestick. There were to be three sets of the three phases of the almond on each branch of the Candlestick, and one of each phase on the main branch and base. That makes nine ornaments on each of the six branches, and a total of twelve ornaments on the main branch and base. There was a total of 66 almond ornaments on the Candlestick. The main branch along with half of the branches would equal 39; while the remaining three branches equaled 27! There are 66 books in the Bible; 39 in the Old Testament and 27 in the

New! There is no doubt the symbolism of the Seven Branched Candlestick alludes to the Holy Spirit and, most certainly, the Word of God!

> [11]Moreover the word of the LORD came unto me, saying, Jeremiah, what seest thou? And I said, I see a rod of an almond tree. [12]Then said the LORD unto me, Thou hast well seen: for I will hasten my word to perform it. — JEREMIAH 1:11-12

God has directly compared His Word to that of an almond tree. There is certainly enough Scriptural evidence to support the Tree of Life being an almond tree. Christians have long associated the cross with the Tree of Life. I believe there is a prophetic connection between the Tree of Life, the almond tree and the cross!

THE CROSS

As we progress into the study of the Cross, please keep in mind that Jesus came to fulfill all Law and Prophecy (Matthew 5:17). A beautiful and glorious thing begins to unfold when you see Jesus in the light of His Word, as the Aleph Tav (the first and the last).

When the soldiers came to arrest Jesus, Peter pulls out his sword to fight. However, Jesus tells Peter to put away his sword and then He makes the following statement in regards to His death:

Thinkest thou that I cannot now pray to my Father, and
he shall presently give me more than twelve legions of
angels? But how then shall the scriptures be fulfilled, that
thus it must be? —MATTHEW 26:52-54

Before they ever took Jesus into custody, He makes it clear that He
had the power to escape but wouldn't. His reason was so that *"the scriptures be fulfilled"* (v. 54). If Jesus was to fulfill the prophecies of His death,
He could not have been slain by just any means. There were many prophecies laid out in the Old Testament that pointed to His death with great
description. Even the Law testified of what manner of death He should die.

Many have the idea that Jesus was crucified solely by the methods of
the Romans. Based on the Scriptural account of the crucifixion, that is
not completely true. The chief priests made it clear that He was to be executed based on their law.

The Jews answered him, We have a law, and by our law he
ought to die, because he made himself the Son of God.
—JOHN 19:7

The Jews had already declared their desire to stone Him for making
Himself one with God. They considered His claims to be the Son of God
to be blasphemy, which would merit stoning under the Levitical Law. See
Leviticus 24:16.

> I and my Father are one. Then the Jews took up stones
>
> again to stone him. Jesus answered them, Many good
>
> works have I shewed you from my Father; for which of
>
> those works do ye stone me? The Jews answered him,
>
> saying, For a good work we stone thee not; but for blas-
>
> phemy; and because that thou, being a man, makest thy-
>
> self God. —JOHN 10:30-33

One would think that Jesus would have been executed by stoning. This was the penalty of the Law. The attempt and desire was witnessed in John 10:30-33. Stoning was not the case. Since Jesus was taken during Passover, it was not lawful for the chief priests to carry out such a judgment which explains the following:

> Then said Pilate unto them, Take ye him, and judge him
>
> according to your law. The Jews therefore said unto him,
>
> It is not lawful for us to put any man to death: That the
>
> saying of Jesus might be fulfilled, which he spake, signi-
>
> fying what death he should die. —JOHN 19:31-32

Jesus knew what manner of death He would die. He had already made it clear that He would be *"lifted up."* He alluded to it early in His ministry when He made this statement:

111

And as Moses lifted up the serpent in the wilderness, even so must the Son of man be lifted up: That whosoever believeth in him should not perish, but have eternal life.
—JOHN 3:14-15

Here Jesus compared His death to the serpent that Moses had lifted on a stick. Allow me to elaborate on this for a moment. Moses had lifted a brazen serpent in the wilderness that brought healing to anyone who looked to it. Bronze in Scripture represents judgment. The serpent being made of bronze represented judgment. This was a reflection of the prophecy God made in Genesis 3:15 where He stated that He would judge the serpent. The picture of a serpent on a stick is wide-spread today whether you have noticed it or not. It is used as an emblem in the medical field. Most would be familiar with it as it is used in relationship to money. The dollar sign ($) is actually derived from the same picture as the medical emblem — a serpent on a stick. Think about it; today our health and prosperity are both linked to the serpent (judged) on a stick! This emblem was fulfilled in Christ by His death on the cross!

When you would think that they would have stoned Jesus, under the limitations of the Passover, the chief priests are calling on Pilate to "*crucify him*." This was a manner of execution by hanging on a tree. This type of condemnation fell within the perimeters of the Law.

One might ask, "*Why did Jesus have to die?*" From the very beginning, God placed a judgment on sin. He gave sin a penalty. The penalty was death. The Bible teaches that "*all have sinned*" (Romans 3:23). Mankind faced the penalty of death. For God to be holy and just, He must honor His Word — sin must be judged. However, at the same time, God is merciful, loving, and gracious. By offering Himself as the Incarnate Son of God, He could pay the penalty of sin on our behalf while demonstrating His love and mercy at the same time! *"For the wages of sin is death; but the gift of God is eternal life through Jesus Christ our Lord"* (Romans 6:23). Not only did Jesus have to die (to pay the debt of sin), but His life had to be without sin. *"For he hath made him to be sin for us, who knew no sin; that we might be made the righteousness of God in him"* (2 Corinthians 5:21). From the beginning, when man sinned and the penalty and curse was pronounced, God set a pattern that He would accept the sacrifice of the innocent to cover the sin of the guilty. That pattern seen throughout the Old Testament in the form of a spotless Lamb was fulfilled in Jesus! Not only did Jesus die to pay our debt of sin, but He bore the curse of the Law as well by hanging on a tree. Truly, Jesus makes us free indeed (John 8:36)! Through Christ, God's mercy and justice were satisfied. *"Mercy and truth are met together; righteousness and peace have kissed each other"* (Psalms 85:10).

Under the Law of the Old Testament, when one was found worthy of death, their body would be hung on a tree. This was an act that portrayed the *curse of the Law*. Deuteronomy 21:22-23 declares that the one worthy of death be *"hung on a tree."* Some have viewed this form of death to be cursed because it prevented the subject from falling on his knees to repent of his sins. In order for Christ to fully redeem us from the curse of the Law, He had to bare that curse on our behalf — He had to hang on a tree (Galatians 3:13). I recognize that one could be hung on a tree after death (by stoning) to fulfill the curse of the Law as well. But it is vital to see that the curse of the Law for the penalty of death was to be hung on a tree. I believe many have missed this aspect of the Law. We can't limit the method of the Roman Crucifixion to the story of the cross. His death and the means of His death fulfilled Old Covenant Law!

> And if a man have committed a sin worthy of death, and he be to be put to death, and thou hang him on a **tree**: His body shall not remain all night upon the tree, but thou shalt in any wise bury him that day; (for he that is hanged is accursed of God;) that thy land be not defiled, which the Lord thy God giveth thee for an inheritance.
> —DEUTERONOMY 21:22-23 (emphasis added)

> Christ hath redeemed us from the curse of the law, being made a curse for us: for it is written, Cursed is every one that hangeth on a **tree**: —GALATIANS 3:13 (emphasis added)

After questioning Jesus, Pilate declared, *"I find in him no fault at all"* (John 18:38). Pilate wanted to release Jesus but the chief priests would not have it. The chief priests and officers cried out saying, *"Crucify him, crucify him"* (John 19:6). Pilate washed his hands before the people and declared that he was *"innocent of the blood of this just person"* (Matthew 27:24). He then makes the statement, *"see ye to it"* (v.24).

> When Pilate saw that he could prevail nothing, but that rather a tumult was made, he took water, and washed his hands before the multitude, saying, I am innocent of the blood of this just person: see ye to it. — MATTHEW 27:24

Because of the Passover, the chief priests of the Jews did not want to perform the execution of Jesus. They insisted that it be carried out by the Romans (John 18:31). Again, it is important to note that a Roman execution did not necessarily mean that He was not condemned in a fashion that would satisfy the judgment of the Law. The chief priests obviously had intimate knowledge of the Law. They knew that the judgment for *"one worthy of death"* was to be cursed by hanging on a tree. Thus, they declared, *"Crucify him."* Notice that only four days earlier the Jews were proclaiming *"Hosanna"* as Jesus entered Jerusalem. I do not believe it's accurate to make the Jews solely responsible for the crucifixion of Jesus. However, the chief priests and officers of the Jews were the accusers and ultimately the ones who brought the condemnation. Peter credited the chief priests with the act of crucifying Jesus when he addressed them.

> The God of our fathers raised up Jesus, whom ye slew and hanged on a tree. —ACTS 5:20

115

Against popular and traditional opinion, I believe that it is highly probable that Jesus was crucified on a literal tree. If you wish to hold to the traditional view of a literal pole with a cross beam, you are entitled to do so. But ask yourself on what evidence you have built your view. Before you dismiss my position, consider the pages ahead. I believe if you built an image in your mind of the crucifixion, basing it solely on what you read in the Scriptures, you might walk away with a different view. Please let me present to you why this is important. In order to see the beauty of His Passion, we need to pull together everything that we have discussed in regards to Jesus, the manifested Word of God, from Genesis to Revelation. As we move forward, keep in mind the Tree of Life, the almond rod (tree), and the cross. Let's begin with Jesus' account of the crucifixion.

> [31]**For if they do these things in a green tree, what shall be done in the dry?** [32]And there were also two other, malefactors, led with him to be put to death. [33]And when they were come to the place, which is called Calvary, there they crucified him, and the malefactors, one on the right hand, and the other on the left. —LUKE 23:31-33 (emphasis added to Jesus' words)

Jesus here says that the "*tree*" was "*green*" (v.31). The word 'tree' is taken from the Greek word '*xulon*,' meaning tree, staff or wood. The word 'green' is taken from the Greek word '*hugros*' which means fresh, sappy or green. It's obvious that this tree is alive; especially by the next statement,

116

"what shall be done in the dry (tree)?" History teaches us of the hundreds that were crucified in 70 A.D. by the Roman army on literal (dry) 'crosses.' Josephus tells us that when the Romans were besieging Jerusalem in 70 A.D. the Roman general Titus, at one point, crucified five hundred or more Jews a day. In fact, so many Jews were crucified outside of the walls that *"there was not enough room for the crosses and not enough crosses for the bodies"* [ELAVIUS JOSEPHUS, Wars of the Jews 5:11.1]. If we begin to build our own image of the crucifixion based on the accounts of Jesus and the disciples, there is irrefutable evidence that the tree appears to be green or alive.

I recognize that many view the "green tree" as Jesus. I have it heard it said that Jesus was calling Himself the green tree as a sign of His innocence (a proverbial expression) —the dry being 'guilty.' Reference has been made to Ezekiel 20:47 to defend this interpretation. In other words, Jesus was saying that if they would do this to an innocent man, what would they do to the guilty? However, we might walk away with a different view of the cross if we took Jesus' words literally — that the cross (tree) itself was green or alive.

When John speaks of the Tree of Life in the Book of Revelation (22:2), it is important to note that the same Greek word for *"tree"* is used — *xulon*. This is the same word used by Jesus when describing the tree that He would be nailed to in Luke 20:31. The word *'xulon'* (tree) is never used in the New Testament to define a wooded pole in the ground. The word *'xulon'* always speaks of a literal tree. It is also the same word used in the following accounts of the crucifixion:

The God of our fathers raised up Jesus, whom ye slew and hanged on a **tree**. —ACTS 5:30 (emphasis added)

And we are witnesses of all things which he did both in the land of the Jews, and in Jerusalem; whom they slew and hanged on a **tree**: —ACTS 10:39 (emphasis added)

And when they had fulfilled all that was written of him, they took him down from the **tree**, and laid him in a sepulchre. —ACTS 13:29 (emphasis added)

Who his own self bare our sins in his own body on the **tree**, that we, being dead to sins, should live unto righteousness: by whose stripes ye were healed. —1 PETER 2:24 (emphasis added)

In each of the accounts listed above, the word *"tree"* is translated from the same Greek word, *xulon*. Again, this is the same word used to describe the Tree of Life in Revelation 22:2. In Hebrew, the same word would be *'ets* (derived from *'atsah*). This is a word used for 'gallows' in the book of Esther where Haman is 'hanged' on a tree (see Esther 5:14; 8:7). My point is that those who gave an account of the crucifixion in Scripture described it as a *"tree."* The original language of the New Testament supports this.

You may be asking, *"What about the cross?"* The word *'cross'* is translated from the Greek word, *stauros*, which means, a pole or cross. The *"cross"* represents the cross-bar (patibulum) that would have been nailed to the tree. Jesus' hands (wrists) would be nailed to the cross when raised up on the tree. We can see that the cross was separate from the tree by the following account:

> And as they led him away, they laid hold upon one Simon, a Cyrenian, coming out of the country, **and on him they laid the cross**, that he might bear it after Jesus. —LUKE 23:26 (emphasis added)

It was on this cross that the inscription, *"Jesus of Nazareth the King of the Jews"* was attached. Can you see Jesus nailed to the cross and then lifted to hang on a tree? Let's keep building on this image.

> And Pilate wrote a title, and put it on the cross. And the writing was, Jesus of Nazareth the King of the Jews. — JOHN 19:19

Before we go any further, let's pull some things together. God has compared His Word to an almond or almond tree. There is no doubt that the original Garden was known for the almond and that the almond was the *"first fruit"* and therefore Holy. As we have discovered in this study, Jesus is the Word. Therefore we can compare Jesus to the fruit of the almond (the first fruit, the fruit of the Tree of Life). With that in mind, let's view the cross as the Tree of Life — a tree with the fruit of an almond (the Word, Jesus) on it! Notice the following prophecy of Jesus given by prophet Jeremiah:

> But I was like a lamb or an ox that is brought to the slaughter; and I knew not that they had devised devices against me, saying, **Let us destroy the tree with the fruit thereof**, and let us cut him off from the land of the living, that his name may be no more remembered. — JEREMIAH 11:19 (emphasis added)

In this prophecy Jesus is compared to the *"fruit"* of the tree. In Revelation 22, the Tree of Life is associated with life, healing, abundance, and blessing. Jesus is the fruit of the Tree of Life! When you receive Him, you receive life (eternal and abundant), healing, and blessing!

There's yet another glorious piece to this puzzle. As we discussed earlier in this chapter, the Menorah or Seven-branched Candlestick, was fashioned in the image of an almond tree. It literally had 66 ornaments of the almond crafted on its seven branches. Basically it had one main staff or trunk with six branches. Now I am going to ask you to develop an image that you may have never considered based on the traditional view of Calvary. I want you to see Jesus crucified with the other two malefactors on the same tree! Can you see three "crosses" fastened to one tree? That would literally give one tree six extended branches. Add those six branches to the tree itself and you would have a seven branched almond tree — a perfect picture of the Menorah on the cross of Calvary!

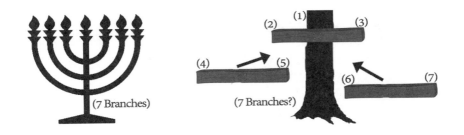

(7 Branches)

(1)
(2)   (3)
(4)   →   (5)
(6)   ↖   (7)

(7 Branches?)

FIGURE 4

Before you abandon the idea, please note that there is no record of three crosses in the Bible. I am not saying there were not three; but notice the following verse:

> The Jews therefore, because it was the preparation, that the **bodies** should not remain upon the **cross** on the sabbath day, (for that sabbath day was an high day,) besought Pilate that their legs might be broken, and that they might be taken away. —JOHN 19:31 (emphasis added)

First of all, the word "*bodies*" is plural while "*the cross*" is singular. It's not wrong to view the tree as a cross. Technically, it is a cross. You have a trunk (pole) and a crossbar, making a cross. In case you are wondering about the two thieves. Notice what the Bible says about Jesus being between two malefactors.

> So the soldiers came and broke the legs of the first, and of the other who had been crucified with him. But when

121

they came to Jesus and saw that he was already dead, they did not break his legs. —JOHN 19:32-33

The soldiers came to the first two thieves and break their legs. But when they came to Jesus, He had already died therefore they didn't break His legs. If Jesus was in the middle of two other crosses, how did they get to Him last? You would think they would have come to Him second; unless they were hanging on the same tree. This would certainly explain how they were able to hold a conversation between the three of them.

Whether it was a literal living tree or a dead wooded post that had been driven in the ground; the point is that Jesus died on a cross (a tree) to redeem us from the curse and penalty of the Law! Whether He died on one of three crosses that day, or if they were all on the same tree, it doesn't take away from the power of His redeeming blood! We may not know every detail of His Passion, but this we know: He bled and died to pay the price of our ransom! The reason I shared these views is to convey to you the beauty and architecture of the Word of God! Jesus did not just happen to die by some undetermined method of death. Everything about His life was declared from the beginning —His birth, teachings, sinless life, death, means of death, and glorious resurrection were all declared beforehand! He is the first and the last; He is the Aleph Tav!

Chapter 7

JESUS: THE AUTHOR AND FINISHER OF OUR FAITH

Looking unto Jesus the author and finisher of our faith;
who for the joy that was set before him endured the cross,
despising the shame, and is set down at the right hand of
the throne of God. —HEBREWS 12:2

I remember as a kid my mom taking us shopping. On many occasions we would pick out our clothes and put them on layaway. My mom would babysit and do women's hair in our home as a means of extra income. She'd take her little extra money and put it towards our items on layaway. My dad worked hard to provide for us and my mom always wanted us to have the best. I can remember going into the store and looking at the coat on the rack and saying, "*I have this on layaway!*" When momma finally paid it off it was an exciting time for my sister and me! I love my momma and am eternally grateful for the sacrifices she made for us. She's in Heaven now and there's not a day that goes by that I don't think of her. My momma loved the Lord. She loved His Word and she loved to hear me share His Word. She loved everyone. I remember her showing love to our neighbors. She was always ministering to others. She's in Heaven today, but not because of the sacrifices she made. Her deeds in this earth were not payments that she made towards her salvation. Eternal life is not a 'layaway' plan that we pay towards with our good deeds. Our redemption was paid in full by Jesus, *the Author and Finisher* of our faith! He is *the first and the last — the Aleph Tav!*

As I shared in Chapter 5, Jesus' last utterance on the cross was, *"tetelestai"* (*"It is finished."*) This word defines a debt being paid. Our eternal redemption is a finished work! Not only is our salvation a finished work, but His promises are also a finished work! See 2 Corinthians 1:20. Faith is a finished work! All that we could ever need physically, spiritually, mentally, and financially has been sealed and provided in Jesus Christ, the Author and Finisher of our faith! He came to give us life and to give it to us more abundantly (John 10:10). Eternal and abundant life is a finished work!

I had a new member of our church share how that at a previous assembly a 'prophet' spoke over her life as well as others in the church. Afterwards, he then informed them that they needed to give an offering in order to 'activate' the prophecy! When she told this man that she didn't have the amount of money he was requesting he told her to write a postdated check! Stories like this grieve me. I can remember seeing a preacher on a Christian television network declaring blessings over his viewing audience. He then claimed that if those viewing would send an offering for a certain amount that they would receive a specific miracle. These 'preachers' give true ministers a bad name!

Jesus doesn't need you to make a payment in order to receive His salvation, power, and deliverance in your life! I am not saying that He won't bless sowing and faithful stewardship. He will. What I am saying is that when He uttered the words, "*it is finished*" from the cross, the debt of our sin was paid in full!

Sadly, there are many who don't realize that Jesus is the fulfillment of all Law and prophecy. His gift of eternal life has been offered by faith. Many view the Law as the means to salvation and are still trying to earn their eternal life. The Law serves as a spiritual mirror. When we look into it, we see our condition. By the Law is the very knowledge of sin (Romans 3:20). You can look into a mirror and see that you are dirty, but that mirror doesn't have the power to wash you — it merely reveals your condition. Jesus came to fulfill the Law on our behalf that by His righteousness, we might be saved!

> Therefore by the deeds of the law there shall no flesh be justified in his sight: **for by the law is the knowledge of sin**. —ROMANS 3:20 (emphasis added)

The Apostle Paul asked the Church at Galatia who had bewitched them. They had come to believe that they were made perfect by the Law. See Galatians 3:1-10. He concluded his point that salvation could only come by faith when he declared the following:

But that **no man is justified by the law in the sight of God**, it is evident: for, The just shall live by faith. — GALATIANS 3:11 (emphasis added)

[19]Now we know that what things soever the law saith, it saith to them who are under the law: that every mouth may be stopped, and all the world may become guilty before God. [20]Therefore by the deeds of the law there shall no flesh be justified in his sight: for by the law is the knowledge of sin. [21]**But now the righteousness of God without the law is manifested, being witnessed by the law and the prophets**; [22]Even the righteousness of God which is by faith of Jesus Christ unto all and upon all them that believe: for there is no difference: [23]For all have sinned, and come short of the glory of God; [24]Being justified freely by his grace through the redemption that is in Christ Jesus: [25]Whom God hath set forth to be a propitiation through faith in his blood, to declare his righteousness for the remission of sins that are past, through the forbearance of God; [26]**To declare, I say, at this time his righteousness: that he might be just, and the justifier of him which believeth in Jesus.** [27]Where is boasting then? It is excluded. By what law? of works? Nay: but by the law of faith. [28]**Therefore we conclude that a man**

is justified by faith without the deeds of the law. —
ROMANS 3:19-28 (emphasis added)

Faith in Jesus is the way to redemption, salvation, forgiveness, deliverance, power, and freedom! When we look into the Word and see Jesus (as the fulfillment of Law and prophecy), we can begin to walk in the power of righteousness that only He can give. Yet sadly, there are many who believe they are making payments on a debt they cannot pay. The wages of sin is death (Romans 3:23). The only payment accepted for sin is death! Jesus has paid our sin debt! We must receive His salvation as a finished work!

Have you ever gone through a drive-thru or a check-out line and realized that you left something behind that you paid for? Maybe you ordered and paid for a combo meal but they forgot to give you your fries. It's aggravating to get home from the grocery store and realize that you left the gallon of milk on the check-out counter. You check your receipt to see if you made the purchase, and there it is on the receipt! The receipt shows that it was paid for but you didn't get it. Well I'm telling you that Jesus has paid for our forgiveness, salvation, deliverance, and freedom. We need to be certain we take home what He paid for! In case you are wondering what He paid for, check the receipt — the Word of God! His Word lists all the things that He has purchased on our behalf!

I love to watch football. I am certainly a fan of the game. In football, a quarterback's rating is effected by the number of passes that he completes. I can imagine how aggravating it would be for a quarterback to place the ball right in the receivers hands but yet they miss the catch. Even though it's the receivers fault, it shows up on the quarterback's rating. I believe the same is true for believers. Jesus has laid His promises right in front of us, yet many are not receiving them. Once we as believers start receiving (catching) the promises that God has given us freely through Christ, our lives will bring Him glory! We can't blame the quarterback (Jesus) when the ball (His promises) was dropped. The Bible says for us to give heed to what we have heard, unless we let them slip (Hebrews 2:1).

LIVING BY FAITH

I have heard it said, *"God said it, I believe it, and that settles it."* Belief is great, and important, but the reality is if God said it, that settles it! Whether we believe His Word or not, He will have what He says. Our faith opens up the power of His Word in our lives. God has called us to live by faith. He has declared that without faith it is impossible to please Him.

Behold, his soul which is lifted up is not upright in him: but the just shall live by his faith. —HABAKKUK 2:4

For therein is the righteousness of God revealed from faith to faith: as it is written, The just shall live by faith. —ROMANS 1:17

But that no man is justified by the law in the sight of God, it is evident: for, The just shall live by faith. — GALATIANS 3:11

Now the just shall live by faith: but if any man draw back, my soul shall have no pleasure in him. —HEBREWS 10:38

But without faith it is impossible to please him: for he that cometh to God must believe that he is, and that he is a rewarder of them that diligently seek him. — HEBREWS 11:6

The faith that God has called us to live by is only found in His Word! Think of it as a literal substance that can only be obtained from hearing God's Word. Romans 10:17 declares, *So then faith cometh by hearing, and hearing by the word of God.* If you polled ten people, you might get ten different answers as to what faith is. There are a lot of misconceptions about it. We can't just generate our own faith. It's powerless. However, there is a faith that has legitimate power. Here is how the Scriptures define true faith:

¹Now faith is the substance of things hoped for, the evidence of things not seen. ²For by it the elders obtained a good report. ³Through faith we understand that the worlds were framed by the word of God, so that things

which are seen were not made of things which do appear.
—HEBREWS 11:1-3

Verse 1 says that faith is *the substance of things hoped for.*" The Amplified Bible reads, "Now faith is the assurance (the confirmation, [a] the title deed) of the things [we] hope for, being the proof of things [we] do not see and the conviction of their reality [faith perceiving as real fact what is not revealed to the senses]." This is the way we have to view faith. It is the assurance, the title deed, the evidence of what we do not see. Faith is the conviction of the reality of what I do not 'yet' see! Keep in mind that *"faith cometh by hearing, and hearing by the Word of God."* The container of faith is the Word of God! Now notice how the Amplified Bible interprets verse 3. "By faith we understand that the worlds [during the successive ages] were framed (fashioned, put in order, and equipped for their intended purpose) by the word of God, so that what we see was not made out of things which are visible." I love that verse! By faith the worlds were framed by the Word of God. We saw that in Genesis; God spoke His creation into existence and laid out the work of the ages through the integrity of His prophetic and infallible Word! By faith God made everything we can see by the power of what we can't see!

Don't be moved by what you see or don't see! The Bible says that God can take the things which "are not" (or can't be seen) to "bring to nought the things that are" (1 Corinthians 1:28). He does this so that no man can boast or glory in himself (v.29). We are the just and we live by faith! *"For we walk by faith, not by sight"* (2 Corinthians 5:7). Make a decision to take Him at His Word. The life of faith begins with hearing and receiving His word. Choose to meditate on His promises and develop an image of their reality in your mind. If you are ever going to see it, you must see it! Imagine His Word coming to pass in your life. Visualize His plan emerging through what may appear to be chaos. No matter how dark the night, hold on to the light of His Word. Hear his Word; meditate on His Word and then confess His Word! Joshua 1:8 declares, *"This book of the law shall not depart out of thy mouth; but thou shalt meditate therein day and night, that thou mayest observe to do according to all that is written therein: for then thou shalt make thy way prosperous, and then thou shalt have good success."*

There's not a more powerful position than for a born-again believer to be declaring the Word of God in the authority of the Name of Jesus! Speak to your mountain. Speak to your circumstances and declare the finished work of Jesus Christ. Once you have heard, meditated, and con-fessed His Word; apply the force of patience. Recognize that when you receive what God has already spoken, that thing is already established in your future! Don't let what appears to be a delay in time hinder your faith. Hebrews 6:12 tells us that it is *"through faith and patience"* that we *"inherit the promises."* What Jesus has started in your life, He will finish. He's not only the Author of our faith; He is the Finisher of our faith! That which He has begun in you, He will finish! (Philippians 1:6).

There are many examples of Jesus being the Author (Aleph) and Finisher (Tav) of faith throughout Scripture. One of my favorites is found

131

in John 11 where Jesus is sent word that His friend, Lazarus, is sick. Jesus' first response was one of faith:

> When Jesus heard that, he said, This sickness is not unto death, but for the glory of God, that the Son of God might be glorified thereby. —JOHN 11:4

You would think that when Jesus heard this news He would immediately go to Lazarus. That is not what happened. The Bible tells us that after Jesus received news of Lazarus's sickness, *"he abode two days still in the same place where he was"* (John 11:6). Though there is a two-day delay, you will see that it does not hinder what the "Author" has said; He declared from the first report that this sickness would not end in death but for the glory of God!

> Then Martha, as soon as she heard that Jesus was coming, went and met him: but Mary sat still in the house. Then said Martha unto Jesus, Lord, if thou hadst been here, my brother had not died. —JOHN 11:20-21

Like Martha, so many times we allow the delay and even the worsening of a situation to convince us that it's over. Here we have two sisters that have reached out to Jesus in regards to their brother's sickness. Not only does Jesus not show up until four days later, but when He finally arrives, their brother is dead!

Jesus had already declared the end from the beginning when He first heard of Lazarus' sickness. Martha's words were, *"Lord, if thou hadst been here, my brother had not died"* (v.21). Likewise, it is said of her sister, *"Then when Mary was come where Jesus was, and saw him, she fell down at his feet, saying unto him, Lord, if thou hadst been here, my brother had not died"* (v.32). To them, it looked to be over; but with God it was not! You see Jesus will always have what He says! Once He says it, it is established at some point in the future. Time only serves as a barrier that doesn't allow us to see with our physical eyes what has already been established! We must learn to be patient and stand in faith in between the promise and the provision. Can we pass the test of faith in the time between hearing and seeing that manifestation of what we have heard?

> Jesus saith unto her, Said I not unto thee, that, if thou wouldest believe, thou shouldest see the glory of God?
> —JOHN 11:40

In response to their doubt, Jesus immediately called their attention back to what He said in the beginning. As the Author, Jesus had already declared what the end would be! He's not just the Author, but He is also the Finisher of faith! The *author* is the *authority* in the matter. Jesus always shows up and manifests His Word in a time and manner that will bring God the most glory! I love this lyric:

133

"Hold on and wait just a little while. He'll bring a song of strength in the midnight. Touch our lives with Your loving Hand. Hold on, we'll hold on." —FRED HAMMOND, "Song of Strength"

Hold on! What can you do with a man that won't quit? I remember one night returning home from ministering at a conference in Texas. On the road that night I decided that I was going to quit the next day. I was discouraged by what appeared to be little results. I had faced this trial and temptation many times but would never act on it. The next morning I got a call from a pastor friend in Dallas who had attended the conference. He called to share with me how encouraged he had been through my radio ministry and Bible Conferences. He had been frustrated and needed strength. He then said to me, *"What can you do with a man that won't quit?"* That statement resonated in me and I have been declaring it ever since!

The trial of faith may be an intense one, but its reward is great and will bring glory to Jesus (1 Peter 1:17)! Remember that the vision of faith is for an appointed time (Habakkuk 2:4) and that there is a time for every purpose under heaven (Ecclesiastes 3:1). We must learn to trust God and wait patiently in faith. As I look back on the hard times of my life and ministry, I am so grateful that the Lord gave me the strength I needed to *"hold on and wait just a little while*!" I am a living witness to the power of faith and patience. God will do what He said He would do! Hold on!

That the trial of your faith, being much more precious than of gold that perisheth, though it be tried with fire, might be found unto praise and honour and glory at the appearing of Jesus Christ. —1 PETER 1:7

For the vision is yet for an appointed time, but at the end it shall speak, and not lie: though it tarry, wait for it; because it will surely come, it will not tarry. — HABAKKUK 2:3

To every thing there is a season, and a time to every purpose under the heaven: —ECCLESIASTES 3:1

I am well aware that sometimes while we are doing all we can to hold on, things can actually get or appear worse! Have you ever called out on God and felt like it only got worse? I remember when we purchased the original property of Word of God Ministries. We were trusting God for the funds to rise and build our first church facility. At that time we were meeting at LSU of Shreveport. We were averaging an attendance record of about 20 — then we got a breakthrough! A building became available which another church had been leasing. We were finally able to move into our own location. Our thought was that by having our own location, we could grow and eventually generate the funds we needed to build on our acquired land. However, a few short months after we moved into the facility, it sold and the new owner required that we vacate. We had more than doubled in size and were seeing growth. This news appeared detrimental to our plans. Here we were trusting God to rise and build and we had just lost what we had. In addition, another church was now occupying space we were leasing at LSUS. I remember that night very well. I went to the pulpit to deliver the news about our having to vacate. Instead, I said, *"Today we received confirmation that we will rise and build!"* I remember us needing roughly $30,000 to start construction. That night we took up an offering and $800 came in. Within a few days our contractor called me up. He heard how we had been made to leave our facility and the Lord moved on him to deduct $30,000 from the contract so that we could begin construction. What appeared to be getting worse actually turned for our good! About six months later we moved into our very own facility. It was a 4,000 square foot facility that would seat about 140. We were full in the opening service and have grown ever since! The reason I shared this is to make this point: no matter what the situation may look like, keep the faith! Jesus is the Author and Finisher of our faith! He is the *Aleph* and the *Tav*! What He has started in you, He will finish!

Abraham was tried when God told him to offer his son. As bad as this may have seemed to Abraham as they traveled up the mountain to the altar of sacrifice, he told his servants that he and his son would return and that God would provide a lamb. We must learn to declare our faith in His Covenant Word! See Genesis 22:5,8. The Scriptures tell of a Shunammite woman declaring *"all is well"* as she was running with her dead child to Elisha, the prophet of God, for a miracle (2 Kings 4:23). She told her servants that she was going to *"run to the man of God, and come again"*

(v. 22). As a result of her tenacious faith, she did just that! Her son was raised to life!

Jesus stepped into a boat and told His disciples, *"Let us pass over to the other side"* (Mark 4:35). That same night a storm arose that literally had the disciples fearing for their lives. They approached Jesus, who was asleep on a pillow, and said unto Him, *"Master, carest thou not that we perish?"* (v.38). They forgot their faith and started to doubt what Jesus had already said. How many times have we wondered what the Lord was doing when things seemed to be getting worse in our lives? I love what Jesus does. He declares what the end will be and then takes a nap! He rests in His Word because He knows He will always have what He says! If only we could learn to rest in His Word! Jesus got up and *"rebuked the wind, and said unto the sea, Peace, be still"* (v.39). I believe here Jesus rebuked the wind and the storm because of its audacity to try and hinder what He had said! Jesus will always have what He says! He is the *Aleph* and the *Tav*, the *First* and the *Last*, the *Author* and the *Finisher* of our faith!

A NEW NAME

How many of us have grown up being called by a name other than the one our parents gave us? In the ninth grade, I had a teacher tag me with the name, *"Hootie."* It stuck with me throughout High School. I have so many friends and acquaintances I know of who are identified by 'nicknames'. Have you ever heard the saying, *"I have a new name written down in glory."*? Well despite what men may call you, when one accepts Jesus

Christ as Lord and Savior, they are given a new identity in Christ. Only, it's not a nickname. It is a new identity that replaces anything we were before salvation. The Bible says old things are passed away and all things become brand new (2 Corinthians 5:17). The new name is a reflection of the "new creation" we become when we accept Christ. Yet, there are many in the Body of Christ who can't see the new nature of a born-again believer. Your new name is the identity of your new nature in Jesus Christ!

There will always be those who want to identify us based on our flesh. Yet the Word says, *"Wherefore henceforth **know we no man after the flesh:** yea, though we have known Christ after the flesh, yet now henceforth know we him no more"* (2 Corinthians 5:16, emphasis added). I'm shocked by individuals who reject an integrated church. As a pastor of a diverse congregation, I witness the prejudice that exists in our communities. It saddens me to see how individuals choose to be plagued by prejudice, separation, and division. We are not to be identified by our flesh. Besides the newness we have in Christ, prejudice is a demeaning and ignorant deception. I've had individuals ask me about the racial make-up of our church as well as ask me how I could pastor a different "race." I tell them that there's only one race — the human race! We may not all look alike, but we were all created of the same blood.

> **And hath made of one blood all nations of men** for to dwell on all the face of the earth, and hath determined the times before appointed, and the bounds of their habitation. —ACTS 17:26 (emphasis added)

Not only will we face those who judge us by the color of our skin; but there are those who will judge us by our past. There are those who come to you in your new-found walk of faith saying, "I know you." You tell them, "You knew me!" Let them know that you have been transformed by the power of Christ! As you renew your mind in His Word, the Bible teaches that your life will transform (Romans 12:1-2). There is a 'newness of life' that believers should walk in (Romans 6:4). Our new name is the mark of a new, born-again, rejuvenated life! Quit identifying yourself with the failures, sin and lifestyle of a life that Jesus has delivered you from! You are not some wanderer roaming around with no purpose. You are an anointed, Spirit-filled, and empowered child of God who has been given an eternal purpose and destiny! You are not an accident — you are a purpose with a name! Before God formed you in the belly, He knew you (Jeremiah 1:5).

The pattern of the name-change in the Old Testament was the addition of the "תא" to the name. We will look at some examples of the name-change in this section. I believe the addition of the *Aleph* signifies that God has called you and equipped you in Christ. The *Tav* represents the mark, plan, and purpose that God has for you! The Father has both called and equipped you to fulfill the purpose He has for you! Things that were not possible without Him become possible with Him! He has signified His plan, power, and purpose in you by giving you a new name (a new identity in Him). 2 Peter 1:3-4 teaches us that God has given us "divine power" that we might walk in a "divine nature." God has put His *super* on your *natural!*

JESUS THE ALEPH TAV

You've got a new name written down in glory! Start walking in your newness! What Jesus the Aleph has started in you, Jesus the Tav will finish in you! The enemy is mad you woke up this morning! You are on a Kingdom-assignment and your new name carries your new power, blessing, and destiny!

> Neither shall thy name any more be called Abram, but thy name shall be Abraham; for a father of many nations have I made thee. —GENESIS 17:5

> And God said unto Abraham, As for Sarai thy wife, thou shalt not call her name Sarai, but Sarah shall her name be. —GENESIS 17:15

> And he said, Thy name shall be called no more Jacob, but Israel: for as a prince hast thou power with God and with men, and hast prevailed. —GENESIS 32:28

There are many name-changes that are clearly seen in Scripture. God changed *Abram* to *Abraham* in Genesis 17:5. Then He changed *"Sarai"* to *"Sarah"* in Genesis 17:15. God changed *"Jacob"* to *"Israel"* in Genesis 32:28. Then there is the New Testament example of where Jesus gave Simon the name *"Peter"* in Matthew 16:18. These are clear and obvious name-changes. In the original Hebrew, Scripture contains an interesting pattern concerning name changes. If you only read the English Translation, you will miss it. There is a pattern in the Old Testament of names being changed once the individual entered into a Covenant of God's Word. I have listed some of these verses below. You will notice that after these individuals entered the Covenant, the (Aleph Tav) "את" was added to their names. Many of these are marriage covenants that portrayed a prophetic line that would bring forth Jesus:

> And Adam knew את-Eve his wife; and she conceived, and
> bare Cain, and said, I have gotten a man from the Lord.
> —GENESIS 4:1

> And they blessed את-Rebekah, and said unto her, Thou
> art our sister, be thou the mother of thousands of millions,
> and let thy seed possess the gate of those which hate them.
> —GENESIS 24:60

It's interesting that when Rebekah is first mentioned in this story in verse 15, there is no (Aleph Tav) "את" connected or in front of her name. But after she was received as Isaac's bride (entering into Covenant with 'Israel'), the (Aleph Tav) "את" appears before her name. So there is a direct connection between ("את") Aleph Tav [Jesus] and the those who enter His Covenant — a literal name change!

> And the young men that were spies went in, and brought
> out את-Rahab, and her father, and her mother, and her

brethren, and all that she had; and they brought out all her kindred, and left them without the camp of Israel. — JOSHUA 6:23

Here is the story of Rahab who is applauded for her faith in Hebrews 11 and shows up in the genealogy of Jesus as well. Rahab is recorded as receiving the messengers of God and rewarded for her faith. She was told to hang a scarlet thread out of her window and that she would be saved when Israel came to take the land by the power of God. This is a picture of the blood that was applied to the doors during the last night in Egypt that caused death to "pass over" the children of God. After Rahab's faith, the (Aleph Tav) "את" is placed before her name for she had entered the Covenant of God by faith!

Moreover את-Ruth the Moabitess, the wife of Mahlon, have I purchased to be my wife, to raise up the name of the dead upon his inheritance, that the name of the dead be not cut off from among his brethren, and from the gate of his place: ye are witnesses this day. —RUTH 4:10

Here, we see Ruth, who also shows up in the genealogy of Jesus, experience this same change in the Hebrew structure of her name. Once she is redeemed by Boaz (a type of Christ), her name has the (Aleph Tav) "את" added to the beginning of it. What's amazing is that each of these women listed above were Gentile women (Gentile meaning they were outside of the Covenant with God) who experienced a name-change and an identity change once they entered into the Covenant. I believe these 'Gentile Brides' of the Old Testament are a picture of the New Testament Church — which is a Gentile Bride redeemed by Jesus Christ!

IN COVENANT WITH ALEPH TAV

The examples of name changes in the previous section of this chapter illustrate the power of the Covenant with Jesus, the Aleph Tav. Within the Hebraic text, a strong covenant is portrayed by a yoke. It is symbolized by placing the *Aleph* (ox head) with the *Lamed* (a shepherd's staff or yoke). So when you see the word "yoke" in Scripture, it can easily represent a covenant between two or more parties. Jesus said, *"Take my yoke upon you..."* (Matthew 11:28). What did He mean by that? He is saying, *"Enter in covenant with me."* He goes on to say that if we take His yoke we will *"find rest unto your souls."* He tells us that His *"yoke is easy"* (verses 28-29). The point is that once in Covenant with Jesus, we can rest! When you enter into a Covenant with Jesus, your soul can rest in His finished work! You can rest that the faith of the Ox (Aleph), has finished the work for your salvation (Tav). Jesus is the Aleph Tav! Not only has He finished the work of our salvation, but also living this life yoked with Jesus makes everything easier! People try to find peace in so many different ways. Only Jesus can give true peace that can't be taken away by anyone or any circumstance. We needn't fear losing it. We can rest in Him.

²⁸Come unto me, all ye that labour and are heavy laden, and I will give you rest. ²⁹Take my yoke upon you, and learn of me; for I am meek and lowly in heart: and ye shall find rest unto your souls. ³⁰For my yoke is easy, and my burden is light. —MATTHEW 11:28-30

A purpose of the yoke was to hook two oxen together. By the power of a yoke, two operate as one! There's power in covenant. Jesus has called us into a Covenant with Him. Therefore, we are no longer alone. In everything that we do, we have His power working with us!

According to the Law, one was forbidden from yoking a donkey *"ass"* and an ox together (see Deuteronomy 20:10). The main reason being that the donkey was more stubborn than the ox. The donkey was also much slower than the ox. If you yoked the two together, the ox would end up dragging the slow and stubborn donkey. Think of an ox as a believer, and a donkey as an unbeliever. How many people do you know that have gotten yoked up with an unbeliever who does not have the same potential and power? What ends up happening is that the one ends up having to drag the other. Before you marry, seek God for one who is a believer and one that you can walk in agreement with in the faith. Otherwise, you might end up dragging your *"ass"* (donkey) everywhere!

Thou shalt not plow with an ox and an ass together. — DEUTERONOMY 20:10

Be ye not unequally yoked together with unbelievers: for what fellowship hath righteousness with unrighteousness? and what communion hath light with darkness?
—2 CORINTHIANS 6:14

The Word of God exhorts us not to be *"unequally yoked together with unbelievers."* The Bible says, *"Can two walk together, except they be agreed?"* (Amos 3:3). It is vital to maintain a healthy relationship with other believers and to stray from relationships where Jesus is not the common denominator. This does not mean that we don't walk in love towards fellow man. It just means that we should not enter into covenant (marriage, strong friendship) with those who don't know Christ or live by His Word (1 Corinthians 15:33, 2 Thessalonians 3:14, James 4:4).

It is vital that we understand our Covenant with God. Jesus has offered us this Covenant by the power of His redeeming blood and there are many believers who live day to day beneath its blessing in ignorance. No matter how we may neglect our covenant, God is aware of it and will not forget it!

My covenant will I not break, nor alter the thing that is gone out of my lips. —PSALMS 89:34

He hath remembered his covenant for ever, the word which he commanded to a thousand generations. — PSALMS 105:8

Covenants are essentially 'contracts' that exist between two or more parties. Covenants are designed to amplify strengths and cover weaknesses. A true covenant comes with responsibilities. In the Western culture, there seems to be a lack of understanding and honor when it comes to a covenant. I believe this is due to an age or culture that truly lacks integrity. A covenant is no stronger than the integrity of the person whose words bind it. A contract is worthless if the person who made the agreement won't honor it. A covenant loses its power and effectiveness when one of the parties cannot be counted on. *"Confidence in an unfaithful man in time of trouble is like a broken tooth, and a foot out of joint"* (Proverbs 25:17). Sadly, it is hard to find men and women who honor what they say. How can I put my confidence in someone when they don't come through with what they said they would do? I believe this is why God went to such depths to prove the integrity of His Word. He wants us to know that we can count on Him to do what He said He would do!

> God is not a man, that he should lie; neither the son of
> man, that he should repent: hath he said, and shall he not
> do it? or hath he spoken, and shall he not make it good?
> —NUMBERS 23:19

He is not just the author of His words; He is the finisher of His words! You can count on God to do what He has spoken. One of the beauties of the Bible is to see its integrity from generation to generation. The study of Scripture opens our eyes to see a faithful God that has done exactly what He said. It lets us know that we can put our trust in Him! He is faithful to His Word! He is a Covenant-keeping God and we are secure in His promises.

> For all the promises of God in him are yea, and in him Amen, unto the glory of God by us. —2 CORINTHIANS 1:20

When God appeared to Abraham and began to share all that He was going to do through him, Abraham responded, *"Lord God, whereby shall I know that I shall inherit it?"* (Genesis 15:8). Abraham's question reflected his need for assurance. God's answer came in the form of a blood Covenant. *"In the same day the Lord made a covenant with Abram..."* (Genesis 15:18).

Make a decision to live your life with the knowledge of your Covenant with Jesus. The details of what you have been promised can be found in the Word of God. Recognize that you are not alone in this thing called life! God has gone through immeasurable depths to demonstrate His love and commitment to man. He loves you! He shed His blood and gave His life so that we might be saved. He has given us His Word so that we might have faith and confidence in the Savior of the world! He is who He says He is and we can be all that He has called us to be! See yourself in Covenant with Jesus. He knows you. He has called you "friend." He knows the number of hairs on your head, He knows the time you fall asleep, the second you awake and even your thoughts. You are the apple of His eye. You are in Covenant with the Most High God and He is ever mindful of His Covenant. He remembers His promises and is faithful to His Word!

David was a man that understood the power of his Covenant with God. When he came out to deliver food to his brothers who were fighting the Philistines, he saw their fear of the giant named Goliath. The armies of Israel stood trembling until David walked up. He knew that God had a Covenant with Israel, but Israel was acting out of fear rather than faith in that Covenant. Unwilling to bow to fear, David called Goliath an *"uncircumcised Philistine"* (1 Samuel 17:36). Circumcision was the token of the Covenant — it was a sign of being in Covenant with God. In essence, David was saying, *"This giant is not in covenant with God!"* David was so confident in his Covenant with God that he went after Goliath with a rock and a sling! If only we would act with the same assurance based on our Covenant. If we would see ourselves "yoked" with Jesus we wouldn't walk in the fear of our enemies. I believe David saw that he had an unfair advantage over Goliath! The Bible says in Romans 8:31, *"What shall we then say to these things? If God be for us, who can be against us?"* You are in Covenant with Jesus, the Aleph Tav (the First and the Last). You have an unfair advantage over your enemies and over any situation that has come against you!

FAITH IN JESUS, THE ALEPH TAV

In closing, I want us to examine an event recorded in the Gospel of Mark that will truly increase your faith in Jesus, the Aleph Tav (the Author and Finisher of our faith)!

And, behold, there cometh one of the rulers of the synagogue, Jairus by name; and when he saw him, he fell at his
feet, And besought him greatly, saying, My little daughter
lieth at the point of death: I pray thee, come and lay thy
hands on her, that she may be healed; and she shall live.
—MARK 5:22-23

Jairus was the ruler of the synagogue. He asked Jesus to come to his
house because his daughter was at the point of death. The Bible tells us
that Jesus went with him (v. 24). I love how Jesus responds to our faith.
Jesus had just gotten off a ship and we don't know where He was heading.
However, when this man came to Jesus in faith — Jesus went with him!
Please know that whenever you step out in faith, Jesus goes with you!
Without faith you cannot please Him. He is a rewarder of those who dil-
igently seek Him (Hebrews 11:6).

While in route to Jairus' house, a woman comes on the scene. The
Bible tells us that this woman had an issue of blood for twelve years. She
spent all she had on doctors hoping to get better, but to no avail. She had
no natural hope. When she heard that Jesus was near, she was determined
to get to him. Her mission was only to touch Jesus' garment, knowing that
if she did, she would be healed.

24And Jesus went with him; and much people followed
him, and thronged him. 25And a certain woman, which
had an issue of blood twelve years, 26And had suffered

149

many things of many physicians, and had spent all that she had, and was nothing bettered, but rather grew worse, ²⁷When she had heard of Jesus, came in the press behind, and touched his garment. ²⁸For she said, If I may touch but his clothes, I shall be whole. ²⁹And straightway the fountain of her blood was dried up; and she felt in her body that she was healed of that plague. —MARK 5:24-29

I want you to understand that this woman made a life and death decision. According to the Law, she was not allowed out in public because of her disease. The punishment for breaking that law was stoning to death. Try to see this situation from her eyes. Jesus had the power to restore her life, and Jairus (the ruler/enforcer of the law) had the power to put her to death. Death and life are literally walking side by side, and her life is hanging in the balance of the decision she will make. Will she move in faith to get to Jesus, or will she allow fear to hold her back? She chose to move in faith! This woman had to trust that if she made it to Jesus before she was noticed that she would be safe. There is no doubt that she had complete confidence that Jesus was indeed the Christ, and that He was the way to her healing! She was so sure that she was willing to risk being stoned to death. I can imagine that fear was present but she overcame it. In her situation, how many of us would have given more weight to the fear of Jairus than faith in Jesus? Fear can be broken down as [F] False [E] Evidence [A] Appearing [R] Real. We must recognize our covenant with God and stand against fear.

The next thing I want to point out about this woman is that *"she had heard of Jesus"* (v.27). Remember, faith comes by hearing and Jesus is the Author and Finisher of our faith! The things she heard about Him moved her to believe that all she had to do was touch the hem of His clothes and she would be made whole. This was her confession before she ever pressed in to touch Him. If you have faith in your heart, it will always come out of your mouth (Romans 10:8-10; Matthew 12:34). Read the Word and be filled with faith. Speak in line with that faith.

Matthew 9:20 sheds more light on this story, declaring she touched *"the hem of his garment."* There is something very significant about the hem of His garment. This particular article was one that Jewish males tradition-ally wore draped over the shoulders. It looked like a large scarf or shawl. It was called a *tallit* or a *mantle*. The tallit had four tassels on each corner that served as a reminder of the Law. The mantle would sway as men would walk. (Did you know that the word "law" actually means walk?) Scripture describes the *tallit* like this:

Thou shalt make thee fringes upon the four quar-ters of thy vesture, wherewith thou coverest thyself. — DEUTERONOMY 22:12

[38]Speak unto the children of Israel, and bid them that they make them fringes in the borders of their garments throughout their generations, and that they put upon the fringe of the borders a ribband of blue: [39]And it shall

be unto you for a fringe, that ye may look upon it, and remember all the commandments of the Lord, and do them; and that ye seek not after your own heart and your own eyes, after which ye use to go a whoring: [40]That ye may remember, and do all my commandments, and be holy unto your God. —NUMBERS 15:38-40

The fringes served as a reminder to walk in the Law of God. The single blue ribbon represented the fulfillment of the Law. There are cases throughout Scripture where we see the mantle (tallit) serving as a covering or covenant. Jesus rebuked the hypocrisy of the Pharisees for making large the borders of their garments (Matthew 23:5). They made a show of the Law without actually walking in it.

The word *tallit* (pronounced tal-eet) literally means 'little tent.' It served as a prayer closet if you will — a miniature tent of meeting or tabernacle. The word 'mantle' is translated from the same root word as *wings*. I am trying to paint a picture for you to grasp exactly what the woman with this disease was thinking when she sought to touch the "hem of His garment."

She understood that the *hem*, or the fringes, were the finished work of the garment or mantle. When she touched that hem she was exercising her faith in the finished work of the Messiah! She was expressing her belief that Jesus was the awaited Messiah, whose death would fulfill the Law. I believe her faith was generated from the Word of God. The prophet Malachi had already declared that the Messiah would come with "healing in his wings"

(Malachi 4:2). The word "wings" is the same word as *mantle*. This mantle that Jesus wore would sway as He walked, reminiscent of wings. Think of the promises we have by coming under His wings! See Psalms 91. There's significant meaning in that thought. Obviously, God doesn't have wings like a bird, nor did Jesus. When we recite the verse, *"there is healing in His wings,"* did we really picture God with wings? No. These promises speak of the mantle — the *tallit;* that served as a reminder of the Law being fulfilled. The Old Testament mantle was a picture of Jesus! No man ever fulfilled the Law other than Christ.

> But unto you that fear my name shall the Sun of righ-
> teousness arise **with healing in his wings**; and ye shall go
> forth, and grow up as calves of the stall. —MALACHI
> 4:2 (emphasis added)

Just as the Word declared, Jesus showed up with healing in His wings. This woman believed what the Scriptures said. She was willing to take God at His Word. She wasn't the only one that had been healed by touching, or coming beneath, His mantle. The Bible says that many touched his garment and were made whole.

> And whithersoever he entered, into villages, or cities, or
> country, they laid the sick in the streets, and besought
> him that they might touch if it were but the border of his

garment: and as many as touched him were made whole.
—MARK 6:56

The mantle shows up throughout the Old Testament. It is used by Elijah and Elisha to heal, raise the dead, and to part the river Jordan (2 Kings 2:8, 13, 14). Ruth draped Boaz' mantle over her when she sought redemption (Ruth 3:8-9). The mantle also represents the Kingdom (1 Samuel 15:27-28). There is a beautiful picture of life, redemption and a covenant of love coming forth as a result of the mantle in the Book of Ezekiel.

> Now when I passed by thee, and looked upon thee, behold, thy time was the time of love; and I spread my skirt over thee, and covered thy nakedness: yea, I sware unto thee, and entered into a covenant with thee, saith the Lord God, and thou becamest mine. —EZEKIEL 16:8

What a beautiful picture of God's mercy and love for us! From the very beginning, God has sought to cover our shame. God's first words to fallen man where, *"Where art thou?"* when Adam was hiding in shame because of his nakedness. Immediately we witness God sacrifice a lamb to cover him. No matter what you are facing; no matter what may be in your past; God seeks to cover you! He will cover your shame through the covenant of His Son, Jesus Christ!

I don't know what caused the disease for the woman with the issue of blood. I can't imagine what her isolated life was like. She had spent all her money on physicians and was no better. Not only was she sick, but she was broke — until she stepped out in faith! On the day of her deliverance she went from being called "woman" to "daughter!" This broken woman found *wholeness* through faith in Jesus, the Aleph Tav — the Author and Finisher of her faith!

Do you need wholeness? Peace? These words come from the Hebrew word, *shalom*. This word for peace conveys much more than a good attitude about a bad thing. Shalom represents safety, soundness, blessing and *wholeness* in mind, body and spirit (1 Thessalonians 5:23). When this woman touched Jesus, the Bible says that He felt that virtue had gone out of Him. He turned to see this woman who had withdrawn healing power from Him. As His eyes fell upon her, his position was one of compassion! He said, *"Daughter, thy faith hath made thee whole; go in peace, and be whole of thy plague"* (Mark 5:34). True peace is wholeness and she had just met the Prince of Peace! Like this woman, we too can withdraw virtue, healing, and wholeness from Jesus Christ! We must be willing to set our minds on His Word and live by faith!

> [8]Finally, brethren, whatsoever things are true, whatsoever things are honest, whatsoever things are just, whatsoever things are pure, whatsoever things are lovely, whatsoever things are of good report; if there be any virtue, and if there be any praise, think on these things. [9]Those things,

which ye have both learned, and received, and heard, and seen in me, do:and the God of peace shall be with you. — PHILIPPIANS 4:8-9

It's important to note that many people were thronging (rubbing against) Him that day. Yet not everyone withdrew power and virtue! Jesus asked *"who touched me?"* The disciples response was basically, *"Everyone's touching you"* (v.30-31). Jesus knows those who are truly pressing in by faith in the midst of the crowds of mere spectators. Just because someone else didn't withdraw the virtue for their breakthrough doesn't mean you won't get yours! Press in to Jesus by faith!

Let's not forget about Jairus! While Jesus turned to minister to this woman, Jairus' daughter was still waiting back at his house at the point of death. I can only imagine Jairus' faith being tested when this woman seemed to be delaying his journey.

In moments of crisis, we have a way of putting our needs before all others. I can remember taking our little family dog to a vet while we were out of town one Saturday. She had been hit by an RTV and looked to be on the brink of death. As I rushed into the vet with her limp little body in my arms, the man in front of me panicked. He claimed that his bird had the West Nile Virus and needed to see the doctor first! Thing was, this veterinarian did not treat birds. The man had a small fit right there in line. He was upset that the doctor took our little dog back to the clinic. Thankfully our dog recovered fine. I don't know what came of the bird with the West Nile Virus. My point is, I am sure Jairus was thinking that this woman should get in line; he had come to Jesus first. Don't let delay lead you into denial. God has a way of showing up when He can get the most glory! Jairus had come to the Author; who would prove to be the Finisher of his faith! At this point in the story, someone from Jairus' house showed up with the news that his daughter was dead (v.34). *"As soon as Jesus heard the word that was spoken, he saith unto the ruler of the synagogue, Be not afraid, only believe"* (Mark 5:35). When Jesus got to his house, He called the girl to arise. *"And straightway the damsel arose, and walked; for she was of the age of twelve years. And they were astonished with a great astonishment"* (v.42). Jesus is the first and the last — the Aleph Tav!

Again and again, God has gone to immeasurable lengths to show us the power of His infallible Word! I exhort you to put your faith in Jesus. What man on earth could have fabricated such hidden truths in His Word? The architecture, numeric and ancient meanings, structure, and consistency of His Word all point to an Author who stands outside of time! He is a God who declares the end from the beginning; for He can see both at the same time!

"SAY IN A WORD"

Of all the faith-building testimonies recorded of Jesus in the New Testament, there is one that is unlike any other. This account is one of the most relevant stories in the Gospels. Of all that came to Jesus in faith, there is one man that Jesus commended above them all.

²And a certain centurion's servant, who was dear unto him, was sick, and ready to die. ³And when he heard of Jesus, he sent unto him the elders of the Jews, beseeching him that he would come and heal his servant. ⁴And when they came to Jesus, they besought him instantly, saying, That he was worthy for whom he should do this: ⁵For he loveth our nation, and he hath built us a synagogue. ⁶Then Jesus went with them. And when he was now not far from the house, the centurion sent friends to him, saying unto him, Lord, trouble not thyself: for I am not worthy that thou shouldest enter under my roof: ⁷Wherefore neither thought I myself worthy to come unto thee: but say in a word, and my servant shall be healed. ⁸For I also am a man set under authority, having under me soldiers, and I say unto one, Go, and he goeth; and to another, Come, and he cometh; and to my servant, Do this, and he doeth it. ⁹When Jesus heard these things, he marvelled at him, and turned him about, and said unto the people that followed him, I say unto you, I have not found so great faith, no, not in Israel. ¹⁰And they that were sent, returning to the house, found the servant whole that had been sick. — LUKE 7:2-10

Here is a man that had also heard of Jesus. He had a servant that was sick and sent word to Jesus. Jesus, being moved by his faith, set out for his house. While in route, the man sent word to Jesus basically telling Him that he was not worthy of having Jesus come under his roof. He makes the powerful statement, *"but say in a word, and my servant shall be healed"* (v.7). Look at this man's faith! All he needed was for Jesus to say that his servant was healed — it didn't matter where He stood geographically! You realize just how powerful this man's faith is when you see Jesus' response. *"When Jesus heard these things, he marvelled at him, and turned him about, and said unto the people that followed him, I say unto you, **I have not found so great faith, no, not in Israel"*** (v.9 emphasis added). Taking Jesus at His Word is the greatest act and expression of faith! Jesus has called us to do the same thing. He said, *"If ye abide in me, and my words abide in you, ye shall ask what ye will, and it shall be done unto you"* (John 15:7). This man understood authority and the power of the spoken word. We too must tap the power of this revelation. How many of us would have sent a message to Jesus that He didn't have to travel to our house, but rather just speak the Word over our situations? It takes a strong conviction and complete confidence in the Word of God to exercise this kind of faith. This is why it is vital that we recognize that Jesus is the Word of God. *"For there are three that bear record in heaven, the Father, the Word, and the Holy Ghost: and these three are one"* (1 John 5:7). You cannot separate Jesus from His Word! He upholds all things by the Word of His power (Hebrews 1:3). His Word is His power! The Gospel *"is the power of God unto salvation to every one that believeth"* (Romans 1:16). His Word has the same power today as it did when this man sought it. Hebrews 13:8 declares, *"Jesus Christ the same yesterday, and to day, and for ever."* His Word will never change! Man cannot deny and time cannot dilute the power of Jesus and His Word! That which is eternal cannot age. Psalms 119:160 states, "*Thy word is true from the beginning: and every one of thy righteous judgments endureth for ever.*"

CONCLUSION

Break free from viewing the Bible as some religious handbook. Don't view the Word as a book that is only opened in church or used by preachers. The Bible is a composition of books filled with words that have come straight from the breath of God! God has embedded such truths in His Word and they all point to Jesus, the Messiah of all mankind!

I have heard some voice the idea that because of the Holy Spirit, they don't need the Word (the Bible). They fail to realize that the Holy Spirit works in harmony with the Word. We wouldn't even know of the Holy Spirit had we not heard of Him through the Word of God! Galatians 3:2 teaches us that we receive the Spirit through the "hearing of faith." Jesus connected the Word of the Spirit to Truth. Notice John 4:23-24; 14:17; 15:26; and 16:23. They all speak of the "Spirit of truth." In John 17:17, Jesus defined "truth" as the "word." Born again believers have the Spirit of God living inside of them (1 Corinthians 6:19). The Word of God is alive, and powerful (Hebrews 4:12), and it works in accordance with His Spirit. His Spirit will move just as He did on Creation's dawn to manifest His Word! There is Spirit-power in His Word. He has the power to raise the dead places in us to life! Notice Jesus' proclamation:

It is the spirit that quickeneth; the flesh profiteth nothing: the words that I speak unto you, they are spirit, and they are life. —JOHN 6:63

Jesus said that the Holy Spirit "shall testify of me" (John 15:26). He also said "He shall teach you all things" (John 14:26). The Holy Spirit is the revealer and He is ready to open your understanding to the depths of who Jesus is. As you open the Word of God, ask the Holy Spirit to reveal to you Jesus! See 1 Corinthians 2:9-11. Quit limiting Jesus to the Gospels and recognize that from cover to cover, Genesis to Revelation, He is not only the Word, but the very letters that make up the Word! There are many who are misled due to their limited or skewed view of Jesus. The answer is to know Him through the volume of His Word (Psalms 40:7; Hebrews 10:7).

Make a decision to get in His Word. Jesus said, *"If ye continue in my word, then are ye my disciples indeed; And ye shall know the truth, and the truth shall make you free"* (John 8:31-32, emphasis added). A *disciple* is a disciplined one. It takes discipline to continue in His Word but the rewards include life and freedom! Choose to live by the faith that is only found in the Word of God! If you have not done so, I exhort you to confess Jesus Christ as Lord and Savior of your life. Receive all that He has done for you by faith.

He is who He says He is and He will have everything that He has spoken! His Word endures unto all generations. He is the first and the last, the beginning and the end. He is the Author and the Finisher. Jesus is the

Aleph Tav! *"And this is life eternal, that they might know thee the only true God, and Jesus Christ, whom thou hast sent"* (John 17:3).

SALVATION PRAYER

I f you would like to receive all Jesus has done for you, and make Him the Lord and Savior of your life, please pray this prayer as you place your faith in him:

Lord Jesus, I believe you are my salvation. I believe that you are the Son of God. I believe that you died for me on the cross. I believe that you were raised from the dead and that you are alive today. I ask you to forgive me of all my sin and to cleanse me with your redeeming blood. I confess you as my Lord and my Savior. Thank you for giving me a new life, a new name, and a new identity in you. I am now your child and Heaven is my home. Have your will in my life and use me to advance your Kingdom. In Jesus' Name. Amen.

If you have made a decision to receive Jesus as Lord, we would love to hear from you!

Contact us at:

Word of God Ministries

P.O. Box 17794

Shreveport, LA 71138

email: info@wogm.com | wogm.com

ABOUT THE AUTHOR

James A. McMenis is the senior pastor of Word of God Ministries. He founded the ministry as a weekly Bible study at the age of 22. Through the local assembly, television broadcasts, and conferences, he has dedicated his life to *"Preaching Jesus as the Manifested Word of God!"* He is known for teaching God's Word in a powerful, fresh, and revelatory manner that always leads to Jesus. Through his sincere, engaging and humorous delivery, he captures a very diverse audience. Pastor James resides in Louisiana with his wife and four children.

Follow Pastor James on Twitter @james_mcmenis.

For more information or resources by Pastor James, visit wogm.com.